WHERE WE STAND

WHERE WE STAND

Voices of Southern Dissent

CHARLES BUSSEY   DAN CARTER
CONNIE CURRY   LESLIE DUNBAR
JOHN EGERTON   PAUL M. GASTON
SHELDON HACKNEY   LAUGHLIN MCDONALD
GENE NICHOL   DANIEL H. POLLITT
JANISSE RAY   SUSAN FORD WILTSHIRE

EDITED BY ANTHONY DUNBAR

FOREWORD BY JIMMY CARTER

NewSouth Books
Montgomery

NewSouth Books
105 S. Court Street
Montgomery, AL 36104

Copyright © 2004, 2017 by NewSouth Books. Individual essays are copyright of their respective authors. All rights reserved under International and Pan-American Copyright Conventions. Published in the United States by NewSouth Books, a division of NewSouth, Inc., Montgomery, Alabama.

Library of Congress Cataloging-in-Publication Data

ISBN 978-1-58838-169-9 (trade cloth)
ISBN 978-1-60306-163-6 (trade paper)
ISBN 978-1-60306-164-3 (ebook)

Design by Randall Williams
Printed in the United States of America

". . . dare tell me you have the strength to combat what you find."

— Lillian Smith (1897–1966)

Contents

Foreword .... Jimmy Carter   9

Introduction .... Anthony Dunbar   12

Acknowledgments 18

Confronting the War Machine .... Dan Carter   21

Standing on the Promises: Absolutes and Imagination
    in Southern Religion .... Susan Ford Wiltshire   45

Ignoring Inequality .... Gene Nichol   61

My Yellow Ribbon Town: A Meditation on
    My Country and My Home .... Paul M. Gaston   70

Our Imperiled Union .... Leslie Dunbar   87

Beyond Capitalism .... Janisse Ray   103

Civil Liberties in a Time of Crises:
    The Dark Side .... Daniel H. Pollitt   121

The Intolerable Burden .... Connie Curry   147

A Postcard from Norway: How America
    Looks from Here .... Charles Bussey   155

Democracy Cannot Be Exported If
    It Is Not Secure at Home .... Laughlin McDonald   169

Identity Politics, Southern Style .... Sheldon Hackney   181

The Southernization of American Politics ... John Egerton   197

Notes 224

Foreword

JIMMY CARTER

THE CONTRIBUTORS to this book and I are deeply concerned about the policies of our government and their profound impact, both at home and abroad.

Our country now is unchallenged as the strongest on earth. Militarily, economically, politically, and culturally the United States is the undisputed superpower. What should this mean to the world? Should we be proud and complacent because the military expenditures of the United States equal the military budgets of all other nations on earth? Despite our superpower status, we should not expect to impose our values on others by force of arms. Instead of using these weapons with little restraint, even in preemptive wars, our country should be known as a champion of peace. Whenever there is an altercation in any part of the world, people should expect the United States to exert its maximum and sustained efforts to support whatever peace processes are possible. We should also be known, without equivocation, as the leading champion of freedom, democracy, and human rights. America ought to be in the forefront of protecting the environment. We should be the most generous nation in alleviating suffering and lead by example in every way that represents the finest aspects of the moral and ethical values that have shaped America's history.

Being a super power does not guarantee super wisdom. We have fared best when we have reached out to responsible partners in the international community for counsel, support, and partnership.

Another serious issue is globalization, which has brought great advances to the United States because we were prepared to devise or take advantage of new technological opportunities. The benefits of globalization require us to be accountable to other peoples who sometimes are affected negatively by our success because they lack the resources to compete with us or even the knowledge and ability to cooperate with us.

As the new millennium was approaching, I was asked about what I saw as the greatest challenge facing the world. It is the growing chasm between rich and poor people on earth. The chasm is widening both within individual countries and between the richest and poorest nations.

Extreme inequality is a moral issue. We must not only feel an obligation to help those in need, but should also recognize that inequality can harm the rich as well as the poor. Those who possess great wealth can become fearful of those who have nothing. Poverty, loss of self respect, and hopelessness often lead to despair, resentment, anger, and violence. The rich and powerful can be tempted to suppress the poor in order to keep them from trying to take what is ours. Democracy, peace, and human rights suffer under such conditions. You can see this in the South, in Georgia, in Plains. You can see this in the conduct of the United States today.

JIMMY CARTER, thirty-ninth President of the United States, is University Distinguished Professor at Emory University and chair of The Carter Center.

The writers of this volume are all concerned about democracy and human rights, and they offer wide-ranging and incisive essays. Some are inspiring; some are disturbing. I am sure that readers will be provoked by them and will learn from them, as I have. ∎

Introduction

ANTHONY DUNBAR

THIS BOOK CELEBRATES some valued American principles: promoting the common good, hope for the future, political compromise, fairness to the minority, everybody pulling the same wagon. In the belief that these treasured ideals still matter, this book also condemns international bullying, unrestrained destruction of our natural environment, extreme—and growing—inequality in the means of living, the creation of a permanent underclass, and mean-spirited politics.

Our writers, all Southerners, share the beliefs that the current policies of our national administration sacrifice the interests of the poor and the people who work for a living to the interests of a privileged elite, that the power of money and the military must be tethered, that the natural environment must be sheltered, and that racial justice matters. A common sentiment is dismay at the deepening chasm that now divides America—and specifically the South—into hostile armies whose leaders are fast losing whatever motivation they ever had to pursue compromise and cooperation, and the common welfare. Beyond that, our essayists are steadfast individualists who are hard to put into a single box.

It is right that this is written by Southerners—white Southerners, at that—because the South has contributed disproportionately to the promise for good in our society but also to its sad misdirection.

Out of the suffering of slavery, civil war, and segregation came redemption through the Southern civil rights movement with its message of resistance to injustice, faith in the rule of law, and belief in human nature as a positive force. This Southern promise of a community of equals built upon individual character has been undermined, however, by an abundant crop of reactionary and harsh public officials, some kept at home and some sent from the South to Washington, who support the economics of militarism, energy exploitation, suburban sprawl, callousness toward the powerless, and piety imposed from the courthouse. These particular Southern contributions have darkened our spacious skies.

Where We Stand is addressed to readers who see, and care about, the drift that America has taken, and who have begun to wonder whether this is the country they grew up in, the country they wish to leave to their children. Coincidentally, the writers come from, or have been active in the affairs of, each of the old Confederate states, from the Baptist flatlands of Texas to the enduring Blue Ridge of Virginia. And in addition to being from Southerners, these essays are also addressed to Southerners, who bear more than their share of responsibility for the fix we are in.

It was not the initial intent that this book be written by Southern whites, but we were reminded early on, by one of those invited to contribute, of another lesson of the black struggle for civil rights: that problems created by the white South ought particularly to be addressed by those who spring from that community. The essays that follow are mindful of that guidance.

While not inevitable, some comparisons might be drawn between this collection of essays and the 1930 classic, *I'll Take My Stand: The South and the Agrarian Tradition*. The twelve white Southerners who composed the earlier book praised agrarian, religious, and aesthetic values over industrial and material ones. The writers of this collection, in contrast, praise democratic and human values over imperial and military ones. They have seen combative, boastful, narrow-minded, sly, deceitful, and personable "leaders" aplenty and know how damaging they can be.

As the Great Depression loomed, the essayists in *I'll Take My Stand* believed that if America were to be reconstructed, the South would have to lead. In that, the present writers might concur. But while the "Agrarians," as they called themselves, contested the social goal of "Progress," realistic people today would have to concede that that battle is long lost. It is not the deterioration of humanist and religious values that is to be feared in our attempts to dominate and industrialize nature; the fear today is the total elimination and destruction of the natural world. Furthermore, the road leads not backwards to the plantation but forward toward a day, soon, when the power of guns and money is harnessed and when the poor of many nations can believe that their advancement and our democratic ideals are compatible.

The Agrarians' hope that Constitutional protection for states' rights would help stem the advance of Yankee capitalism has gone the way of the Carolina panther. Some of the writers of the present volume helped to lay that belief to rest, but for the different reason that states' rights was misused to impede racial integration. Likewise, the old claim that life in the Cotton Kingdom had substantial aesthetic value, and that the safe place for African Americans in the South (safe for all concerned) was in agriculture, has been buried—by Southerners mainly, including some of the writers in the pages that follow.

ANTHONY DUNBAR is the Lillian Smith Book Award-winning author of books about Mississippi, Appalachia, migrant workers, and the Southern labor movement, including *Mississippi: Our Land, Too* and *Against The Grain: Southern Radicals and Prophets 1919-1959*.

Railing against industrialization is such a lost cause that it now seems quaint. But the Agrarians were prescient about some things. Every ill perceived by those poetic thinkers—the ever-quickening speed of life, the coarsening of personal expression and public discourse, the loss of leisure, the loss of joy in work, the devotion to money-making—has become so. They were right about that. Those evils now define much of our culture.

What the Agrarians did not see clearly was the power which the United States would achieve. They did not foresee the overwhelming military might, the economic goliath, the grader's power to level mountaintops, the restrictions upon dissent and movement that "Progress" would construct and require. And they did not have the optimism to believe that the broad range of American citizens would correct the country's course, not out of nostalgia for a leisurely world built on the backs of underpaid labor, but out of a belief in the Constitutional, democratic, and therefore inherently revolutionary principles on which our nation was built.

The following essays are structured loosely around these themes. No manifesto accompanies the words. The chapters here are individual expressions of concern about the gap between where America is and where it should go. There is no yearning here for an easier day, when challenges were few, because the concept of "America" has always been a challenge to oppression and a call to inevitable and unending struggle to defend freedom. Each of the contributors to this book, in his or her own voice, speaks, out of the Southern experience, to that America.

The Southern experience makes one wary of self-righteousness, and these Southerners are alarmed (and think the reader also must be) about the rise of evangelical fundamentalist influence in government at all levels, and the threat this trend presents to the constitutional principle of separation of church and state. No one can appreciate those dangers more acutely than a Southerner. The precarious hold that so many Americans have on a job, a home, and three meals a day is also especially evident in the South.

The Southern liberal tradition out of which this book springs teaches other lessons as well. Always a minority force—whether speaking against slavery, segregation, or the oppressiveness of a society in which power and privilege reign supreme—progressive voices in the South have learned that opposition to injustice is a hard duty, not an enjoyable right. They have learned from the leadership of Southern blacks that the misuse of power must be attacked frontally.

Their topics here range from DAN CARTER's confronting the war machine that led us into Iraq to DANIEL H. POLLITT's review of the consequent loss of our civil liberties.

GENE NICHOL speaks of the perils of ignoring growing inequality in our economic life, and SUSAN FORD WILTSHIRE shows how the Bible itself is a subversive influence in the South—both for good and for evil.

The danger of forgetting the constitutional promise of a more perfect union is presented by LESLIE DUNBAR, and JANISSE RAY, lamenting our assaults on the natural world and our unsustainable lifestyle, urges that we look beyond industrial capitalism.

PAUL M. GASTON writes of the betrayed dream of the utopian Alabama colony of his youth to illuminate the increasingly endangered American dream, and CHARLES BUSSEY gives us the view from Europe on America's war policies and growing intolerance.

Threats to our democracy at home, including the imprisonment and disenfranchisement of African Americans in the South, are explored by CONNIE CURRY and LAUGHLIN MCDONALD.

The tragedy of Southern politics, and its rise to national dominion, is traced by SHELDON HACKNEY, and by JOHN EGERTON, who declares that all America has now been Southernized.

The state of our union portrayed in these essays is a dark one.

We write in the belief that the more Americans learn about what we believe to be the truths of our condition, the sooner we will be able to reverse the trends. We strive to keep hope alive. There is much we have alluded to only in passing, or have left out altogether, such as campaign finance, the loss of privacy, the giveaway of federal contracts to cronies, and the poverty of public education. We leave ample ground for others to plow. Here is the place where we stand. ■

Acknowledgments

THE AUTHORS gratefully express their appreciation for the keen editorial advice of John F. ("Zig") Zeigler. His efforts have been immensely helpful throughout the process of creating this book. Paul Gaston and John Egerton also read and provided valuable suggestions about many of the chapters as the book was being assembled.

We are grateful to each of the following for their material contributions to this project: Hodding Carter, Leslie and Peggy Dunbar, John Fein, Gareth Gaston, Mary and Paul Gaston, Vernon Jordan, Ret. Admiral Gene La Roque, Priscilla Johnson McMillan, and Boyd Tinsley.

We also appreciate the hospitality of Will and Brenda Campbell, who hosted at their Tennessee farm a retreat attended by most of the authors and editors of the book during its planning stage.

Finally, we wish to acknowledge as well that this book might not have appeared at all, and certainly could not have been presented in a timely fashion, had it not been for the tireless efforts of the staff of NewSouth Books, particularly Randall Williams, a gifted editor with feet firmly planted in the struggles of his native Black Belt, Suzanne La Rosa, our publisher who has made her press a noble voice heard far from its base in Alabama, Michael Reynolds, whose command of the politics of publishing has contributed much to the wide readership this book has already achieved, and Rhonda Reynolds, the talented cover designer who made it all look good. ■

WHERE WE STAND

Confronting the War Machine

Dan Carter

FORTY-EIGHT HOURS before the United States invaded Iraq, I sat in a windowless classroom and listened intently as twenty-seven of my undergraduate students shared their views on the coming war. They were mostly junior and senior history majors, hard-working and intellectually engaged in the course on race and Southern culture. The great majority, and certainly those who were willing to speak, passionately defended the need to wage war.

For almost an hour, they faithfully repeated the justifications offered by the Bush Administration: Saddam Hussein was linked to al-Qaeda; Iraq had huge stockpiles of weapons of mass destruction and was on the verge of building nuclear bombs that would soon be handed over to fanatical "hate-America" terrorists for detonation in the United States; we needed to take firm action because the Clinton Administration had so weakened our military that terrorists and militants felt free to strike without danger of reprisal; the cowardice of Europeans (and the weakness of the United Nations) meant that only the United States could protect itself. After we take care of Iraq, said one of my older students, the United States would have to invade Iran, North Korea, and Syria in order to create democracies like ours.

As they talked, I kept reminding myself that these were the voices of mostly young people in a very conservative state, in a city that is home to one of the largest military training centers in America. But it was still unnerving to listen as only one individual—a twenty-year-old Scottish exchange student—challenged these pro-war arguments and pointed to the dangers that this preemptive and unprovoked attack on Iraq posed for world peace.

Any illusions I once held that the United States was uniquely virtuous vanished long ago. But through the years I have retained a belief that America's historical experience—the longest of any existing democratic republic—offers people around the world something greater than efficient washing machines and state-of-the art advertising campaigns. Just as the French Revolution, for all its excesses, held out the promise of a new way of thinking (liberty, equality, fraternity) the American experiment offered other nations a flawed model, but a model nevertheless, of how constant democratic renewal might keep in balance the forces of personal liberation and social responsibility.

When my students had spoken, I urged them to think about the consequences of our actions and to question the hubris that is involved in the notion that we can reshape the world in our image.

I don't think I made much headway. And I shouldn't have been surprised.

Millions of Americans opposed the war with Iraq in the spring

---

DAN T. CARTER is the Educational Foundation Professor of History at the University of South Carolina. A past president of the Southern Historical Association, most of his writing has dealt with the intersection of racial, economic, and political issues in American history. His books include *From George Wallace to Newt Gingrich: Race in the Conservative Counterrevolution, 1963-1994; The Politics of Rage: George Wallace, the Origins of the New Conservatism and the Transformation of American Politics; When the War Was Over: The Failure of Self-Reconstruction in the South, 1865-1867;* and *Scottsboro: A Tragedy of the American South.*

of 2003; the demonstrations that sprang up across the country reflected those convictions. But the events of September 11 seemed to have paralyzed much of the nation's established leadership. Even critics of the Bush policy such as the editorial writers of the *New York Times* often seemed to base their opposition on the timing of the invasion, or the failure to wait for sufficient international support. Only a few left-wing journals and marginalized political activists challenged the foundations on which the Bush invasion plans rested. Nor was there any widespread public debate on the dramatic and dangerous implications of the Administration's embrace of preemptive war.

That encounter with my students and their lack of skepticism about the militarization of American foreign policy forced me to consider the possibility that—in the words of the distinguished political scientist and international scholar Chalmers Johnson—we are well on the way to replacing our two-hundred-year-old republic with an aggressive militaristic empire, a "massive military power athwart an angry, resistant globe." And it has led me to try and understand how this has happened and how we might yet change course.

IN LATE 2003, the Congress of the United States approved a Bush Administration defense budget of $365 billion and a supplemental appropriation of $87 billion for operations in Afghanistan and Iraq. That total did not include $10 billion for missile defense appropriations, $18 billion in the Energy Department budget for nuclear weapons, $30 billion for "Homeland Security" and $30–35 billion for the secret "black budget" of the Central Intelligence Agency and other intelligence operations. (These covert budgets, by law, are barred from scrutiny by the taxpayers of the United States.) With the bipartisan approval of these appropriations, the United States has become responsible for nearly fifty percent of the world's military expenditures.

Even as the defense budget increased dramatically between 2001 and 2003, state and local governments faced a combined budgetary shortfall of $200 billion. Faced with an electorate that seemed unwilling to consider tax increases and constitutional restrictions that (unlike the national government) forbid long-term borrowing, political leaders responded by cutting health care, welfare benefits, education, the arts, public safety, the transportation infrastructure, and other essential public services. By the beginning of 2004, Alabama had placed its highway patrolmen on a four-day work week. Nationally the number of poor people who lost their health benefits as a consequence of state budget cuts reached more than one-and-a-half million. California alone faced a budget deficit of $14 billion. If these reductions heightened the pain caused by the economic downturn of these years, the Bush Administration's Pentagon planners felt no constraints. They outlined future increases calling for military expenditures of well over $500 billion annually by 2008, double the spending in the last years of the Clinton Administration.

Americans were told that these increases were essential to protect American security. George Bush seemed unable to speak in public without warning of the need for a strong military to protect America against a repetition of the nightmare of September 11. In justifying its budgetary requests for 2004, the Department of Defense repeatedly invoked the "threat of terrorism" as a key factor in the need for such dramatic increases. The department's web page lists as its first priority the support of the President as he "wages war on terrorism—terrorism both at home and abroad." But even a cursory examination of the Pentagon's budget shows that the bulk of these escalating expenditures are for elaborate weapons systems useless in confronting the asymmetrical national security threats we are likely to face in the years ahead. In August of 2003, for example, the Navy Department approved the purchase of six nuclear-powered attack submarines for $8.7 billion as part of a ten-year program to acquire thirty additional nuclear-powered submarines at a minimal cost of $80 billion.

At a time when no potential opponent is developing major weapon systems, it would seem self-evident that the nation's security will not be significantly enhanced by spending billions of dollars for nuclear submarines, surface vessels, the Navy's "Super Hornet," the Air Force's F-22 "Raptor," the F-35 Joint Strike Fighter, the V-22 Osprey, and other staggeringly expensive high-tech weapons delivery systems. Guarding against terrorist attacks remains the primary function of intelligence agencies and state and local law enforcement agencies. Should a terrorist incident occur, the primary response would come from overburdened and underfinanced state and local governments and federal agencies outside the Defense Department. Five or fifteen or fifty missile-carrying submarines will do nothing to stop a suicide bomber or a group of airline hijackers.

If our armada of supersonic aircraft, ponderous motorized artillery, and high-tech weaponry is often irrelevant in the struggle to control international terrorism, it is easy to see why this war machine is so politically popular. After declining in the aftermath of the Vietnam war, defense expenditures increased dramatically in the 1980s, more than doubling in the Reagan Administration. With the collapse of the Soviet Union in 1991, the much hoped-for "peace dividend" proved illusory; a generation of Cold War spending had created a momentum that defense contractors and their conservative supporters shrewdly maintained with skillful lobbying, well-placed campaign contributions, and a strategic dispersal of pork as they spread subcontracting production facilities for weapons systems across the congressional districts of key Republican and Democratic legislators. These tactics seem to have made bloated and wasteful defense programs immune from the rigorous scrutiny that has characterized conservatives' oversight of benefits for poor or working-class Americans.

The makers of the B-2 bomber, one of the weapons systems vigorously promoted by the Reagan Administration, originally promised to produce each aircraft for $550 million. The B-2 bomber ended up costing $2.2 billion, by weight more expensive than if it had been made of solid gold. After it was built, the aircraft proved extraordinarily difficult to maintain and so expensive that they were seldom used in combat. As the humorist Dave Barry noted, however, it had one effective merit: its "breathtaking capability, unmatched in aviation history, to deliver, with pinpoint accuracy, extremely large payloads of taxpayer dollars into the districts of strategic members of Congress."

If little of the expected post-Cold War peace dividend materialized, there was a modest decline in defense expenditures during the Clinton years. Between 1990 and 1997 appropriations went down nearly 25 percent in real dollars. And there seemed a growing consensus among knowledgeable defense analysts for the elimination of major Cold War weapons systems. In the months leading up to the presidential election of 2000, Donald Rumsfeld—then George W. Bush's primary advisor on defense matters—spoke often about the need to phase out projects that made no strategic sense in a post-Soviet era. After September 11, however, such rhetoric faded as the Bush Administration sought to avoid any opposition from within the defense establishment and embraced many of the weapons systems that Rumsfeld had originally questioned.

As the defense budget ballooned, the GOP's emphasis upon privatization (a process begun in the Reagan and first Bush administrations and continued through the Clinton years) has allowed defense contractors to reap even greater profits as they increasingly assume functions once restricted to uniformed military support units. Peter Warren Singer, a security analyst for the Brookings Institution, has shown how such Fortune 500 companies as Halliburton-Brown & Root and Dyncorp have erased the divide between the military and the corporate sector. Between 1994 and 2002, private contractors who replaced military and defense department personnel received more than $300 billion in government contracts; in 2003 alone, such corporate warriors—most of them American—had worldwide revenues of $100 billion.

As the initial fighting in Iraq wound down in late April and early May of 2003, the media raised questions about the political connections of private contractors that were likely to become involved in the postwar reconstruction of Iraq. But the reality is that they were on the ground from the beginning, maintaining military aircraft and ships and supplying food and water and other logistics to American forces (often very poorly). Little wonder that the *Economist* magazine called the 2003 invasion of Iraq "the first privatized war." Not surprisingly, these defense contractors have tended to show their gratitude at election time. The millions of dollars in campaign contributions passed on to the current White House occupant and other Republican and Democratic politicians is a minor-add-on to the cost of doing business.

Outsourcing national security responsibilities to private corporations whose primary allegiance is to increasing profits may benefit politicians, but it is fraught with long-term dangers to our political system and the well-being of our armed forces. It is also an invitation to the inevitable corruption that flows from such crony capitalism. As the reconstruction of Iraq began in the late spring and early summer of 2003, five major companies—Halliburton, Bechtel, Fluor, Parsons, and the Washington Group—received billions of dollars of noncompetitive contracts and placed themselves in a commanding position to receive the lion's share of the $100 billion that will be spent rebuilding that war-torn country. And what do these companies have in common? They are politically well-connected and they have given lavish political contributions to the Republican party. To paraphrase (and to contradict) the famous line by General Motors CEO Charles Wilson ("What's good for the country is good for General Motors, and vice versa"), what is good for Bechtel is *not* necessarily good for the country. And the incestuous revolving door by which ex-military officers, former government officials and political figures move seamlessly between public positions and private employment in these defense industries is simply one more example of the corruption inherent in the process.

Financial fraud and political corruption are, however, the least of the problems posed by the new American militarism. What we *must* understand is the connection between its destructive power abroad and its debasement of American values at home.

REPRESENTATIVES OF THE BUSH Administration saturated the air waves with apocalyptic warnings of imminent "mushroom clouds" and powerful visual representations of tiny test tubes of biological agents that supposedly could kill millions of Americans. In the months after the war was declared to be over, investigative reporters, led by Seymour Hersh writing in the *New Yorker,* began to expose the many ways in which the White House had deliberately misrepresented intelligence data. Much was made of the President's use of crudely fabricated documents purporting to show that Hussein sought to obtain "Niger" yellow cake uranium. But that falsehood was only the tip of an iceberg of deception.

In January of 2002, when UnitedNations officials privately informed Washington that Hans Blix would lead an inspections team into Iraq, Assistant Secretary of Defense Paul Wolfowitz ordered the C.I.A. to investigate what he insisted was the Swedish diplomat's failure to detect secret Iraqi nuclear activity when he was chief of the International Atomic Energy Agency (IAE) during the 1980s and 1990s. (Blix, in fact, readily acknowledged that he had been deceived by the Iraqi government.) But the C.I.A. report concluded that Blix had failed to detect Iraq's nuclear violations primarily because of limitations placed upon him by the IAE. According to a State Department official, Wolfowitz "hit the ceiling" over the failure of the C.I.A. to come up with evidence to discredit Blix. In the time between Blix's appointment and his team's eventual withdrawal from Iraq, the Administration—particularly staff members for Wolfowitz, Vice President Cheney, and Donald Rumsfeld—developed what the *Guardian* called a systematic whispering campaign impugning Blix's integrity, working through such favorite news outlets as the *Wall Street Journal,* the *Washington Times,* and sympathetic columnists. ("Hans Blix is Saddam Hussein's man," reported one conservative columnist with particularly close contacts in the White House.) Only in June 2003 after the fall of the Hussein government, did the urbane diplomat finally vent his anger in a British newspaper interview, lashing out at the "bastards" in Washington who had "spread things around. . . , who planted nasty things in the media."

Neither Bush nor Cheney nor any of the other Administration representatives had to defend their deceptive statements during the run-up to the war. While the print media hardly distinguished itself, television networks essentially became official conduits for official propaganda. And it is television that increasingly "informs" Americans on issues of international affairs and domestic politics. In the months leading up to the war and during the conflict itself, a Los Angeles *Times* poll found that 12 percent of the American people rely primarily upon print media for news, 18 percent upon traditional broadcast news sources, and nearly 70 percent upon Fox News, CNN, and MSNBC. Jeff Cohen, a senior producer at MSNBC, put it best: "The ideologues in the Bush White House apparently learned from watching the rise of Limbaugh and Fox News: When you invert or concoct reality, do so passionately and repetitively, and accuse anyone who challenges your reality of liberal bias . . . or treason." With the exception of a few gadflies like Ted Koppel of ABC News and programs on PBS's "Frontline" series, there were few such challenges from television broadcasting. George Bush and other Administration figures were free to spread misleading information without concern that they would be contradicted.

America's media has seldom played a critical role in challenging national policy, particularly in times of war and heightened tension. After Woodrow Wilson successfully obtained the Declaration of War resolution in April of 1917, few voices questioned America's decision to join the conflict. Certainly there were none after Pearl Harbor. In the Cold War atmosphere of the 1950s, the news media never challenged official policy regarding the Korean War. (The only debate revolved around whether we should use nuclear weapons, as General Douglas McArthur demanded.) And even though we often associate the Vietnam War with a critical press, not one reputable reporter questioned the truth of the nonexistent North Vietnamese attack on American ships in the Bay of Tonkin in 1964 that served as a justification for the passage of the "Tonkin Gulf Resolution" and led to America's disastrous intervention in that war. Only the growth of a significant anti-war movement in 1966 and 1967, coupled with the shock of the Tet Offensive of January 1968, led a growing number of reporters to question the Johnson Administration's assurance that there was light at the end of the Vietnam tunnel. As one combat correspondent later concluded, in every conflict, the media "parrots back the clichés and jingos of the state. In wartime, the press is always part of the problem."

What is different is the level of sophistication this Administration and its supporters have brought to the task of manipulating public opinion. It is not hyperbole to say that they echo George Orwell's dystopian novel, *1984*. In the aftermath of September 11 the carefully marketed television coverage bore more than a passing resemblance to the "Oceana" in which Big Brother constantly bombarded frightened inhabitants with lies and deceptive propaganda, justifying a state of continuous war.

The coverage of the war itself was a particularly repellant reflection of the media's subservience to Administration policies. Relatively few British and American soldiers died in the first weeks of combat and the several thousand Iraqis who perished remained largely invisible because of the decision of the networks to minimize coverage of civilian casualties. (The few newspapers that broke that pattern soon retreated in the face of furious assaults by readers who demanded that they stop undercutting American morale.) "Operation Enduring Freedom," a brief and decisive assault by America's overwhelming forces against a hapless and depleted army, allowed television networks to transform bloodshed into spectator sport, a high-tech video game in which death was seldom allowed onscreen and the good guys always won. Day after day, news announcers, studio military "experts," and embedded reporters offered viewers the emotional comfort of jingoistic patriotism, introduced at every stage with stirring musical soundtracks and brand-name logos wrapped in waving American flags: "A Nation United"—ABC News; "America Fights Back"—CBS News; "America Strikes Back"—MSNBC and Fox News Channel. The actors in this televised production seldom deviated from a script that could have been—and often was—written by the Pentagon. Even the use of the terms "America Strikes Back" and "America Fights Back" confirmed the Administration's argument that the war against Iraq was in retaliation for the Hussein government's connection with the September 11 terrorist attacks.

Twenty years of covering global conflicts convinced *New York*

Times war correspondent Chris Hedges that waging war created a corrupting death spiral from which neither victim nor perpetrator escaped. But in his book, *War Is a Force That Gives Us Meaning*, Hedges recognized the seductive power of "that process of dehumanizing the other, that ecstatic euphoria in wartime, that use of patriotism as a form of self-glorification, that worshiping of the capacity to inflict violence—especially in a society that possesses a military as advanced as ours."

In 1914, German soldiers marched off to the First World War with *"Gott mit uns"* (God with us) stamped on their belt buckles. Publicly, no one in the Bush Administration described the war as an instrument of God's will, but the President sought at every point to convince Americans that this nation was the embodiment of all that was decent, honorable, and noble, while its opponents ("evildoers," "terrorists," "mass-murderers," "thugs") deserved only to be obliterated. And privately, according to Palestinian Prime Minister Mahmoud Abbas, Bush claimed a higher authority. "God told me to strike at al-Qaeda," Bush told Abbas, "and I struck them, and then He instructed me to strike at Saddam, which I did."

WITH GOOD REASON, much has been made of the duplicity of the Bush Administration, but the major outlines of these militaristic policies have remained, like Edgar Allan Poe's purloined letter, in plain sight. *New York Times* columnist David Brooks, panderer George Will's successor as the spokesman for the respectable right in America, has dismissed descriptions of the connection between the Bush Administration's policy and neo-conservative thinkers like Paul Wolfowitz, Richard Perle, Doug Feith and Bill Kristol, and Norman Podheretz. Brooks refers to such linkages as examples of anti-Semitic conspiracy-mongering by deranged liberals who are the left-wing equivalent of radical right ideologues raging against the Trilateral Commission. But describing how these ideologues have created a rationale and justification for a new imperial America is neither anti-Semitic nor a reflection of conspiratorial assumptions. In a March 2003 essay in *Washington Monthly*, Joshua Micah Marshall described with meticulous detail and considerable restraint the role these neoconservatives played through the 1980s and 1990s in constructing an ideological framework of assertive military interventionism. Vice President Cheney and Defense Secretary Rumsfeld share their views. It is equally clear that their ideas appealed to a president with only the most shallow knowledge of world affairs, a tendency to see complex issues in simplistic terms ("You're either with us, or you're against us . . .") and an apparent belief that God had chosen him to bend the Middle East to America's will and reshape it in our image: "democratic," pro-American, and economically accessible and responsive to the interests of American-led multinational corporations.

In the aftermath of World War II, presidents from Harry Truman to Bill Clinton sought to project American power and economic interests by building (and dominating) a complex and advantageous network of international arrangements and institutions. There have been important exceptions to this internationalism: in Vietnam in the 1960s, for example, and in the Western Hemisphere where the United States has repeatedly asserted its economic and military hegemony. By and large, however, this policy worked to the benefit of American strategic and corporate economic interests. In his June 2002 West Point graduation speech, George Bush, however, proclaimed a dramatic departure from traditional American foreign policy and international law. The United States military was "ready to strike at a moment's notice in any dark corner of the world." America's security "will require all Americans to be . . . ready for preemptive action when necessary to defend our liberty and to defend our lives." Four months later, the Administration unveiled its "National Security Strategy" which formally embraced the doctrine of preemptive wars and put the rest of the world on notice that the nation would tolerate no significant military opposition. With astonishing hubris the National Security Council announced that there was a "single sustainable model for national success": the United States. Ex-diplomats and scholars of international politics generally reacted with dismay at what they saw as the reckless and self-defeating implications of Bush's embrace of preemptive war. But once again the television networks (and much of the print media) gave only passing notice to this dramatic departure in American foreign policy. Most shameful was the failure of the Congress to debate the long-term implications for the nation. (During the week of October 3–10, 2002, when the Congress voted overwhelmingly to give President Bush open-ended authority to wage war against Iraq, there was no debate on this policy or the implications of the Congress's abrogation of its war-making powers. None.)

Although the Bush Administration sought to depict this policy shift as a necessity in the wake of September 11, its emphasis upon assertive unilateralism predated these events. The refusal to respond to international concerns over land mines, the overt hostility to attempts to strengthen international law through the World Court and the withdrawal from the Kyoto protocol negotiations on global warming all reflected the commitment of a leadership intent on asserting a Pax Americana through military superiority.

Many factors have led to this shift in American foreign policy. For some supporters of the Administration, maintaining (as they see it) the security of Israel is critically important. Others see the creation of an overwhelming military superiority as essential to protecting and projecting American economic interests abroad. For still others, there is the belief that overthrowing repressive regimes like Iraq's will set off a chain reaction of democratization in the Middle East and other parts of the world.

But we should not overlook the obvious. By insisting scornfully and repeatedly that energy issues were irrelevant in making the decision to invade Iraq, the Bush Administration succeeded in discrediting critics who blamed oil companies. But, whatever one may think of Assistant Secretary of Defense Paul Wolfowitz, we should be grateful for his candor on this subject in the immediate aftermath of the war. For "reasons that have a lot to do with the U.S. government bureaucracy," he told an interviewer in March 2003, "we settled on the one issue that everyone could agree on: weapons of mass destruction." When asked a month later why a nuclear power such as North Korea was being treated differently from Iraq, where there were (in fact) no weapons of mass destruction, Wolfowitz minced no words. "Let's look at it simply. The most important difference between North Korea and Iraq is that economically, we just had no choice in Iraq. The country swims on a sea of oil." At Bill Clinton's impeachment trial, former Arkansas Senator Dale Bumpers recalled H. L. Mencken's observation that "When somebody says it's not about money, it's about money." Well, said Bumpers, "When the House lawyers say this isn't about sex, it's about sex."

And this is about oil.

WITH EVERY PASSING DAY, we can see the price we pay for this military adventurism. Americans have been fixated upon the growing number of American casualties, but the number of Iraqi civilians killed in the war and in the war's aftermath have now reached between eight thousand and ten thousand deaths with another twenty thousand wounded.

And what of our position abroad? In 2002, on the eve of the full-scale campaign to build support for an Iraqi invasion, pro-American attitudes in France, Britain, Germany, Italy and Russia ranged from 61 to 75 percent. By the time the first rockets fell on Baghdad in March 2003, the Pew Research Center for the People and the Press found a precipitous decline in positive global attitudes toward the United States. Nowhere in Europe was there a majority that regarded the United States favorably; only in Britain did more than a *third* of the people express positive views about our nation. Six months after the fall of Saddam Hussein, new polls by the Pew Center and the Marshall Fund of America found even greater misgivings about American foreign policy and its role in the world, nowhere more so than in the predominantly Muslim world. (In Turkey, pro-American attitudes plummeted from 50 to 12 percent; in Indonesia from 61 to 15 percent.)

If we are paying a price abroad for our reckless policies, the cost at home is equally high. The continuing cost of maintaining this vast military—when coupled with the Bush Administration's trillion-dollar tax cuts for the wealthy—conveniently reinforce conservative demands that nonmilitary expenditures be "restrained." Behind a facade of "compassionate conservatism," the Bush Administration moves by stealth toward the goal bluntly outlined by conservative ideologue Grover Norquist: gradually reducing the federal government's social programs until they can be "drowned in a bathtub." In the short term, George W. Bush is lavishing funds on favorite constituencies in the run-up to the 2004 election, but social and environmental programs are being starved. And, when the bills come due, they will suffer even more.

The events of the last two years have again reminded us that war is always the enemy of social justice in a democratic society. But this Administration already has earned a special place in historical infamy for its willingness to engage in what Nobel laureate George Akerlof has called "a form of looting" as it mortgages our future with its shortsighted economic policies and militaristic adventurism.

For those of us who support the broad goals of a humane social democracy, it is particularly painful to watch Bush Administration policies seek to unravel a safety net slowly constructed over much of the last century. As we transfer trillions of dollars in tax revenues to the rich and billions of dollars to weapons of mass destruction, public schools cut short their academic year, colleges, universities and trade schools raise their tuition, and the number of uninsured Americans rises past 41 million as cash-strapped states enact new measures to eliminate the desperate poor from Medicaid rolls. No one said it better than President Dwight Eisenhower a half-century ago. "Every gun that is made, every warship launched, every rocket fired signifies, in the final sense, a theft from those who hunger and are not fed, those who are cold and not clothed." A world in arms was "spending the sweat of its laborers, the genius of its scientists, the hopes of its children."

ANALYZING AND DESCRIBING THE CRISIS we face is easier than offering a way out.

It is easy to see why many Americans who are part of the long tradition of liberalism are paralyzed by the sense that nothing can be done to reverse the direction of American policy. While almost any Democratic alternative is preferable to the current administration, we should not underestimate the extent to which both political parties are complicit in their subordination to moneyed interests and their unwillingness to challenge our country's growing emphasis upon military solutions to every challenge. At the same time, the very nature of the political and economic structure makes it difficult to imagine mounting a sustained opposition political movement from within American society.

There is, first of all, the difficulty of reaching an electorate increasingly dependent upon a television "news" system that offers little insight into our current crisis. The news divisions of the television networks are simply revenue-producing subsidiaries of huge multinational corporations. General Electric owns NBC and MSNBC; ABC is under the entertainment umbrella of Walt

Disney, Inc.; Time-Warner owns CNN; CBS is under the aegis of the giant entertainment firm, Viacom; and of course Rupert Murdoch runs Fox News as part of his far-reaching right-wing propaganda machine. (All 140 of Murdoch's newspapers around the world supported the war in Iraq.)

Underlying this media embrace of the status quo is the larger context in which wealthy American conservatives have reshaped the battleground of ideas. As late as the mid-1960s, American liberalism, with its emphasis upon moderate social policies at home and American-dominated internationalism abroad, still shaped the parameters of public debate. Beyond the *National Review* (a magazine of decidedly limited circulation), the fringe right-wing publisher, Regnery Press, and the editorial pages of a few pro-business newspapers like the *Wall Street Journal*, one would have been hard pressed to find national outlets for the kind of doctrinaire conservative views that now dominate American political and media discussions.

In the last three decades, however, the landscape of American intellectual debate has been transformed by the growth of a vast right-wing media apparatus anchored by talk radio hosts like Rush Limbaugh, but increasingly dominant on "mainline" television media outlets that are now simply a money-making segment of corporate America, an echo of their masters' voices.

There are many reasons for the decline of American liberalism; not a few are related to its own weaknesses. But we should not overlook the behind-the-scenes role played by wealthy right-wing ideologues. Pittsburgh billionaire Richard Mellon Scaife is best known for spending more than two million dollars on the "Arkansas project" to uncover Clinton scandals. (He was particularly intent on proving that the White House had arranged the assassination of Vince Foster.) Less known is the critical role he has played in bankrolling a sophisticated conservative infrastructure: think tanks like the Heritage Foundation, organizations promoting right-wing litigation such as the Pacific Legal Foundation and the Southeastern Legal Foundation, magazines, college newspapers and other conservative publications. All have benefited from his largesse. By 1998, Scaife had contributed more than $640 million (in 1998 dollars) to these conservative groups. Other wealthy donors like Colorado beer brewer Joseph Coors, oil man Fred Koch, Vicks heir H. Smith Richardson, Jr., and former Treasury Secretary William Simon also recognized the powerful role their contributions might make in building an infrastructure to promote right-wing ideas throughout the nation.

At the same time, the sclerotic nature of American politics makes it difficult for voters to have an impact upon the levers of political change. It is not simply the enormous influence exerted by powerful economic interests: the very nature of the system itself seems impervious to challenge. In 1962, more than a third of the seats in the United States House of Representative were considered competitive from election to election. By 2002, skillful gerrymandering by the two political parties meant that 190 Republicans and 166 Democrats won reelection by margins of more than 20 percent. Less than 10 percent of the seats were truly open to challenge and that percentage was declining with each new reapportionment bill in the nation's state legislatures.

Perhaps most discouraging is the fact that—despite clear disagreement on specific issues by much of the electorate—George W. Bush retains the support, admiration, and confidence of a great number of voters. For those on the left, it is difficult to see how anyone could find comfort in the rhetoric of this inarticulate Texas trigger-happy cowboy. Within a week of September 11, Bush called for the apprehension of Osama Bin Laden "dead or alive," with a clear preference for the former. His bluster soon echoed through his Administration. The State Department's coordinator for counter-terrorism gave a reporter his recipe for killing Osama Bin Laden and then confirming his death to the world. "Take a machete and whack off his head, and you'll get a bucketful of DNA. . . . It beats lugging the whole body back!"

A substantial minority of the nation's citizens have been repelled by this, the language of the swaggering schoolyard bully, and see it as a reflection of the coarsening of our foreign policy and our values as a nation. But not the majority of Americans. While polls are notoriously fickle and prone to shift from week to week, throughout much of 2003 and into 2004, they showed a relatively consistent pattern: Americans were skeptical of Bush's handling of the economy, but by a 2-1 margin they consistently saw him as a leader likely to protect the nation against terrorism. On the surface this seems absurd; even poll respondents suggest that the nation is *less* safe from terrorism than before the September 11 attack. This disconnect between our growing insecurity and faith in the Administration's leadership has led scholars and pundits—particularly on the left—to offer explanations for this apparent contradiction.

Renana Brooks, a clinical psychologist with an interest in political leadership, has suggested that Bush's fundamental appeal lies in his Administration's manipulation of the nation's fearfulness, a manipulation using linguistic techniques borrowed from generations of advertisers who have understood the role of fear and uncertainty in manipulating consumers. First, there is the insistence that we are in a permanent state of crisis, a war without end. As Bush said in a television speech immediately after September 11, "Americans should not expect one battle, but a lengthy campaign, unlike any other we have ever seen." Some might ask: "how urgent this danger is to America and the world," he said a month later. "The danger is already significant, and it only grows worse with time." Unlike earlier presidents who had balanced warnings of danger with optimistic rhetoric, Bush constantly focused upon the perilous future. With the nation on edge, he repeatedly used "catastrophic words and phrases," argued Brooks, until Americans felt such a "high level of anxiety" that it appeared pointless to respond constructively to the threat. With each new high-profile alert, with each warning of the potential for imminent disaster, the tendency has been to cede power to the President as a strong and forceful leader willing to strike back against the nation's tormenters.

George W. Bush certainly sees himself as that strong father figure. As he told *Washington Post* reporter Bob Woodward in the aftermath of September 11, "I'm the commander—see, I don't need to explain—I do not need to explain why I say things. That's the interesting thing about being president. Maybe somebody needs to explain to me why they say something, but I don't feel like I owe anybody an explanation."

Our task is to recognize that this Administration's foreign and domestic policies abroad are of a piece. The dismissal of the Kyoto Accords is inextricably linked to the relentless war on our own environment; the Bush Administration's refusal to acknowledge the rule of international law is matched by its contempt for civil liberties at home; its insistence that all nations accept our version of unfettered corporate capitalism is part and parcel of its domestic worship of the marketplace, its deliberate encouragement of growing inequality, and its war on the social institutions that lie at the foundation of a decent social democracy.

The duplicitous justifications for this administration's foreign policies are matched by its Orwellian rhetoric at home. Political leaders have always sought to present their policies in ways that appealed to voters, but none have matched the manipulative cynicism of this Administration. Proposals to privatize (and thus destroy) Social Security and Medicare are inevitably packaged as "reforms." "Leave No Child Behind" is announced with great fanfare and then dramatically underfunded. When all else fails, Bush policymakers simply misrepresent the truth. When Secretary of Labor Elaine Chao introduced a plan to change the rules on overtime pay, she claimed that an additional 1.3 million workers would receive overtime pay while the plan might make 644,000 workers ineligible. An analysis by economists for the Economic Policy Institute, a liberal but highly respected think tank, found that as many as eight million workers would be barred from overtime while fewer than 700,000 low-income workers would be made eligible.

But nothing is as reflective of such "doublespeak" as the Bush Administration's environmental "reform" proposals. In 2002, citing the damage inflicted by the summer's forest fires, President Bush introduced his "Healthy Forests Initiative" which he promoted as a means of protecting communities and homes from future conflagrations. Private logging companies would be given access to the nation's forests to engage in "fuel reduction" while incidentally marketing enough timber to make their efforts worthwhile. In fact, as attested by every independent forestry researcher, such logging actually *increased* the danger of fires. The proposal was simply a cover to allow logging companies to enter federal lands and harvest large fire-resistant trees, valuable commercial timber, and old-growth forests. When the Congress failed to enact the measure, President Bush adopted it by executive fiat.

In 2001, the Environmental Protection Agency proposed a replacement for the existing Clean Air Act that would place a greater reliance upon the cap and trade credit system of regulating pollutants. Many environmental groups cautiously welcomed the EPA's proposal. But by the time the Bush Administration had introduced its "Clear Skies Initiative," it had so modified the EPA proposal that the measure's results would have led to far worse pollution than under existing legislation. By the fall of 2003, more than 1,200 community groups and environmental organizations had come out in opposition.

Recognizing the challenge we face should not lead us to despair or to exaggerate the extent to which our freedom to think and act is threatened. The Patriot Act adopted in the panicky aftermath of September 11 is a travesty of American principles and the federal government daily abuses the constitutional rights of the nation's citizens and the norms of civilized behavior in dealing with noncitizens. But George Bush is no dictator and the United States is far from a totalitarian society. If Fox News (and to a lesser extent the other broadcast networks) are little more than megaphones for the Bush Administration's repeated misstatements and tortured logic, the truth is readily available. While the print media plays a diminished role in the nation's civic dialogue, the cumulative impact of investigative reporters (however belated) in the wake of the war and the increasing role played by internet groups like MoveOn.org are slowly—ever so slowly—forcing into view the profound deceptions that have marked the Bush Administration.

The real danger we confront is not the likelihood that we will be directly intimidated by John Ashcroft's Justice Department, but the temptation to retreat into self-censorship and passivity. In 1956, in a different and yet similar time, *New York Times* publisher Arthur Sulzberger described the Cold War's "smoke screen of intimidation" that had stifled essential debate and created a "fog through which we wander uncertainly." But it wasn't the "superzealots" who concerned him, he said: "it is the lack of plain old-fashioned guts on the part of those who capitulate to them."

In the end, there is no silver bullet, no well-marked roadmap to lead us out of this wasteland of fear and self-deception. What we have to remember is that authentic political movements begin at the grass roots level and have their greatest impact when we least expect it. Who could have predicted the great achievement of Social Security in 1929? And who could have anticipated in 1948 that we were on the verge of an all-out assault on segregation? The women and men who challenged Jim Crow in the 1930s and 1940s faced obstacles as great as any we now confront. It is always difficult to predict where, when, or how the next movement against militarism and social injustice will coalesce and emerge, but we have to learn from our mistakes, build upon our defeats, and move forward with the kinds of arguments and proposals that may seem futile at the moment. ■

Standing on the Promises: Absolutes and Imagination in Southern Religion

SUSAN FORD WILTSHIRE

Poet and critic Allen Tate, the only one of the Vanderbilt Agrarians I was in time to have met, wrote in his essay on religion in *I'll Take My Stand* (1930): "Abstraction is the death of religion as well as of everything else."

Tate identified the peril of absolutist religious beliefs. Absolutes are abstract. They have to be. Life actually lived is far too messy to be subject to human absolutes of any kind, particularly in matters of religion. Absolute premises exclude those who fail to "measure up" to predefined requirements.

This leaves two possibilities about the nature of God: a God who is exclusive or a God who is inclusive. For absolutists, God excludes from grace those who are defined as outside the kingdom. In the more ambiguous and hospitable notion of a loving, inclusive God, there is room in the kingdom for everybody: We are all sinners, and God loves us anyway.

Thomas Merton puts it this way: "A holy zeal for the cause of humanity in the abstract may sometimes be mere lovelessness and indifference for concrete and living human beings. When we appeal to the highest and most noble ideas, we are more easily tempted to hate and condemn those who, so we believe, are standing in the way of their realization."[1]

These two strands have long coexisted in Southern religion. Both were shaped during the same years in the same part of my world: west Texas in the 1950s, '60s, and '70s.

AT A LUBBOCK, TEXAS, high school reunion, I found myself visiting with two friends from those long-ago days. After a while one man explained to the other: "Susan became a liberal because she went to New York."

I smiled meekly and nodded. (Old habits are hard to break.)

No, I thought to myself. I became a liberal because I went to church.

The influence was indirect. In those years I never heard a prophetic word uttered from the pulpit about race or McCarthyism or the death penalty or nuclear war or anything else of the sort. Rather, church formed the habits of my heart. For me its disciplines included reading the Bible through; memorizing Bible verses; attending Sunday School and church youth groups; and earnest projects of personal piety. On weekdays I attended Morning Watch, a Protestant worship service with hymns and prayers held in the public school auditorium each day before classes.

Church in all these forms instilled in me a sense of fairness, a passion for justice, and the faith and words to fuel them both.

SUSAN FORD WILTSHIRE is a native of Texas. She has lived and worked for thirty-five years in Nashville, Tennessee, where she is chair of the Department of Classical Studies at Vanderbilt University. Her books include *Public and Private in Vergil's Aeneid*; *Greece, Rome, and the Bill of Rights*; *Athena's Disguises: Mentors in Everyday Life*; *Seasons of Grief and Grace: A Sister's Story of AIDS*; and *Windmills and Bridges: Poems Near and Far*.

What I would not know until much later was that in the same time and place, representatives of my own denomination were propagating a very different kind of religion.

In high school in 1957, it was my responsibility to invite speakers for school assemblies. For our annual "Brotherhood Week" in February, I asked a minister of one of the more open-minded denominations in Lubbock to be our speaker. He agreed and then asked what he should talk about. I would be embarrassed to remember exactly how I phrased it, but it was something like "I guess about our getting along with colored people."

The big day came. The pastor spoke for half an hour. He never ventured anywhere near the subject of race. I was puzzled and surprised by his avoidance.

LONG BEFORE MY GENERATION knew what a Movement was or even that there was a need for one, we learned our first Movement song in Vacation Bible School:

> Jesus loves the little children
> All the children of the world;
> Red and yellow black and white
> They are precious in his sight.
> Jesus loves the little children of the world.

The subversive truth was already there. It all seemed so simple.

That these words took root in my consciousness was a result also of the home in which I was raised. When I was in the sixth grade, my mother invited the principal of my nearby elementary school together with Mae Simmons, the principal of the segregated African-American elementary school across town, to come to our house for tea. My mother had met Ms. Simmons in one of her volunteer activities and thought the two principals would have much in common and would enjoy meeting each other. The year was 1952. This may have been the first integrated social occasion in my town. As we drank our tea around the fireplace, three of us were having a very good time. The white principal sat mute and agitated.

In that moment I realized something was very wrong in our society.

By the time I went to the state university in Austin, many people knew something was wrong. In 1959 the few African-American students at the University of Texas could not participate in intercollegiate sports. They could not belong to the band or work in the library. They could not see a movie or buy a sandwich or get a haircut anywhere near the campus.

I joined the Student YMCA/YWCA and found myself challenged by a faithful community to participate in the stand-ins and picket lines that in time changed these ironclad customs. In those years I learned two important lessons: 1) faith without action is feckless, and 2) you can be right, or pretty sure you're right, and people can still hate you. Until then I thought that if you tried very hard to be good, people would like you.

Doug Rossinow describes the radicalization of students in the mid-sixties at the University of Texas in *The Politics of Authenticity* (1998). I am grateful I graduated and left Austin for New York in 1963. Soon thereafter the pietist nonviolent movement for integration gave way to a more anarchic confluence of drugs, sexual revolution, and protest. Given my natural reserve I would have found it hard to steer between the Scylla of my straightness and the Charybdis of my convictions. Much to my amusement, my name appears twice in Rossinow's book: once connected with a prayer at the installation of new Y officers, then again describing my pathetic efforts at diplomacy when the Dallas *Morning News* accused the Y of being a Communist front. To this day I still ask anyone who generalizes about the sixties, "Which sixties do you mean?"

Then came Vietnam.

It all seemed so simple.

"Blessed are the peacemakers." "Thou shall beat thy swords into plowshares."

I joined a few antiwar marches in New York in my years in graduate school at Columbia University, but these were peaceful until the spring of 1968. By that time I had been gone almost a year.

I will never forgive Lyndon Johnson for squandering on his deadly exercise of military machismo far from home the resources that could have funded a better society at home. At least two lieutenant colonels in Vietnam, Colin Powell and Norman Schwarzkopf, saw the awful consequences of civilian leaders playing military and military leaders playing politics. They vowed we would never make the same mistake again.[2]

And now, with the U.S. invasion of Iraq in March 2003, we made the same mistake again. This time the consequences are far more ominous. Wars of preemption are now official U.S. policy, which means a perpetual state of war including the potential use of nuclear weapons. The moral, geopolitical, and budgetary costs are already catastrophic.

The ancient Romans had a similar policy. Every time they invaded another country, they declared war with a ritual prayer to Jupiter and Janus and "all the other gods." The historian Livy gives the exact wording: that whatever people the Romans are invading at the time "are unjust and have not rightly paid us our due" [*iniustum esse neque ius persolvere*] (*A.U.C.* 1.32.) And so the invasions began.

But I get ahead of myself.

THEN CAME THE WOMEN'S MOVEMENT.

It all seemed so simple. At first.

Sometime in the early seventies I was invited to participate in a radio debate with a woman representing the then-fashionable notion of "total woman." This idea was promoted in a book advising women to be submissive to their husbands and to welcome them at the door upon their return from work clad in plastic wrap. Thirty-nine scriptural references in the book supported the subordination of women. I pointed out that one important passage, Galatians 3:28, had been omitted: "There is neither Jew nor Greek, there is neither slave nor free, there is neither male nor female; for you are all one in Christ Jesus." (RSV).

"Christianity was good for women." This observation by my high school Latin teacher was lodged in my memory. In time I learned enough about the Greco-Roman petri dish in which Christianity grew to understand why this might be the case. I learned also that the apostle Paul's imprecations against women occur mostly in his letters to the Corinthians—inhabitants of the only site in the Greek world where temple prostitution was practiced. Paul had something else in mind for "religious women."

When I moved to Nashville in the fall of 1969, I understood that Vanderbilt did not hire women. I was not dismayed by this and did not even question it. That was the way Aristotle created the universe. Fortunately I was hired as director of the Honors Program at Fisk University. I am grateful for that wonderful job for many reasons, one being that it allowed me to remain in my beloved profession of teaching.

By the time I joined the faculty of Vanderbilt University in 1971, the women's movement was well enough under way that students soon came to ask my help in organizing a Women's Studies course. I told them I was not interested and, in any case, it would take two years to get a new course through the curriculum. They got the course underway the next semester without my help. Within months, my views had changed and I became active in the movement for women's studies and women's equity at Vanderbilt. A decade later this led to a very contentious lawsuit in federal court. I was not the plaintiff, but I was one of the more visible supporters of the brilliant young English professor who was.

This time, the conflict affected me right in the center of where I live and work.

This time, it hurt.

This was when I learned that if we remain faithful enough to institutions to try to change them, they will break our hearts.

Most of my male colleagues and one or two of the handful of women on the faculty took the other side. "You have a good issue," one dean said to me, "but this is not a good case." Another admired colleague told me he was afraid he might never be able to speak to me again. For three years I woke up most mornings rehearsing speeches and devising strategies for our campaign. We formed WEAV (Women's Equity at Vanderbilt). We raised $65,000 to fund the lawsuit.

We lost the case.

We won the cause.

Now, more than two decades later, Vanderbilt University is a delightful place for most people to work. Childcare centers, parental leaves, and an outstanding program in Women's Studies benefit men as well as women. And what happened to the plaintiff Elizabeth Langland, whose feminist research was considered "not scholarly" by the dean who refused her promotion? Six books and two good jobs later, she at this writing is Dean of Humanities and Fine Arts at the University of California, Davis.

Another more personal result was this: Until my work with WEAV I did not believe I could write a scholarly book. After confronting those in power at my institution, I lost my fear not only of academic power-holders but also of two thousand years' worth of scholars in my field of Latin literature. Eleanor Roosevelt said that only those who are without fear can be full of mercy and grace and generosity. Only those who are not afraid are free. The day the lawsuit began, I began in earnest writing my first book.

THEN CAME SEXUAL ORIENTATION.

It all seemed so simple. This time it was not optional.

In 1980 at the age of thirty-four, my handsome, successful, compassionate younger brother John Edward Ford told me he was gay. I was four years older, but we were so close our father called us littermates.

John had been appointed Deputy Assistant Secretary of Agriculture in 1981, the highest position he could seek without Senate confirmation, which might have uncovered his sexual orientation. When he died of AIDS in 1993, he left unfinished the novel he was writing about gays in the Reagan administration. While I was looking for a writer to complete John's manuscript, a mutual friend introduced me to Mel White, author of *Stranger at the Gate: On Being Gay and Christian in America* (1994). I had breakfast and conversation with Mel and his partner Gary Nixon. The conversation was so happy and animated I felt I had just had breakfast with my brother John, twice.

Mel was conceiving a new interfaith movement called Soulforce that would adopt the nonviolent principles and practices of Gandhi and Martin Luther King in the struggle against anti-gay church policies. Soulforce is committed to ending spiritual violence and hatred perpetuated by religious policies and teachings against gay, lesbian, bisexual, and transgendered people. Mel and I stayed in touch, and before long he called me to say, "I have an idea. I'm thinking about going to Lynchburg, Virginia, to pay a little visit to Jerry Falwell. What do you think about that?" I said, "I have no idea what I think about that. But I'll tell you this: If you go, I'll go."

We went. Before leaving for Lynchburg, two hundred of us studied the methods and spirituality of nonviolence and committed ourselves to those principles. In Lynchburg we were hosted by a hospitable church where we worshiped, prayed, and created a community. We met with two hundred of Falwell's followers in what Falwell originally proposed as dinner but at the last minute devolved into plastic bottles of water, plastic cups, and a plastic dish of ice in the middle of each table.

We were launched. My faith, activism, belief in nonviolence, and passion for justice had found a home together. The discipline of nonviolence does not come easy for me. Left to my own natural Texan instincts, my political activity of choice might be a rattlesnake in the mailbox. Nonviolence demands continuing scrutiny of ourselves and our motives to remain even a little faithful to its spirit and practice. Nonviolence requires never wishing ill on one's opponents. Thomas Merton again is helpful here:

> Christian nonviolence does not encourage or excuse hatred of a special class, nation, or social group. It is not merely *anti*-this or that. In other words, the evangelical realism which is demanded of the Christian should make it impossible for him to generalize about "the wicked" against whom he takes up moral arms in a struggle for righteousness.

In the spring of 2000, the quadrennial meeting of General Conference of the United Methodist Church took place in Cleveland, Ohio. Soulforce had communicated extensively with denominational leaders, hoping they would resist escalation of the church's anti-gay policies. When that approach failed, consistent with Soulforce principles we prepared for a direct action of civil disobedience. We worked in advance with the Cleveland Police Department, which treated us with courtesy and respect.

The arrest, my first, was transformative. To stand charged in front of a judge brought a huge shift in perspective. So did a stay of several hours in the crowded cells of the Cleveland city jail. As the heavy metal door clanged shut behind me, I saw standing in the men's holding cell to my right the Reverend James Lawson, still the stalwart champion of justice he was when he trained students in nonviolence for the Nashville sit-ins in 1960. Next to him stood Gandhi's grandson, Arun.

The acts of civil disobedience and the arrests were the simple part. What broke my heart that day was something else. During one of our training sessions, a Soulforce member described being turned away from membership in a large Methodist church in Kentucky because she is lesbian and open about it. Her pastor preached that homosexuals could not inherit the kingdom of God. He had explained to my friend that he was sorry she had to be penalized for being honest. When she named the preacher, I gasped. He had been one of my favorite students at Vanderbilt.

How had this bright young man and I, from such similar backgrounds, come to such different understandings of our faith? How did it happen that as my faith deepened, my activism for social justice increased, while his views became more rigid and conservative as he grew in the church? How did it come to be that my view of the church is inclusive and his is exclusive?

To my sorrow, the same West Texas culture that formed me also produced a new form of evangelism based on hatred of gays.

IN 1965 I RODE THE BUS home to Texas from graduate school in New York. It was a fifty-hour journey. I woke up in the dark to see an illuminated billboard: "Martin Luther King at Communist Training School."

I knew I was home.

At the height of the Red Scare in the mid-1950s, articles in *Reader's Digest* had attacked the World Council of Churches and the National Council of Churches. During this same period, impassioned anti-Communism in the South often veiled an even more profound racism, as John Egerton relates in *Speak Now Against the Day* (1995). The race card was played again as right-wing religious organizers found that attacking mainline churches and their seminaries was a successful way to attract followers.

Then the race card took yet another face. This time the hatred and fear that propelled movements against integration and the equality of women were aimed at homosexuals. Around 1970, ambitious small-town preachers in the Northwest Texas Annual Conference of the United Methodist Church began to exploit "the gay issue." They saw that virulent anti-gay rhetoric could fill football stadiums for revivals in such tiny Panhandle towns as Tulia and Clarendon and Higgins and Perryton. There it was safe to attack both queers and the national denominations that might welcome them.

From this small start independent ministries eventually flourished. A number of these organizations now share overlapping board memberships with Asbury Theological Seminary in Kentucky and with the national Institute on Religion and Democracy, which attacks mainline churches for their inclusive policies on women and gays and any liberal stands on social questions. For example, the stated purposes of the I.R.D.'s Ecumenical Coalition on Women and Society are these: "1) to reverse detrimental cultural trends, 2) to press for renewal of biblical orthodoxy in the Church, 3) to call for a more central role for faith in society, and 4) to counter radical feminist ideology and agenda." The I.R.D. is heavily funded by the Scaife Foundation.

Asbury Theological Seminary has close ties to Methodism

but opposes the national organizations of the United Methodist Church. Methodist founder John Wesley held a four-fold test for truth—reason, authority, scripture, and experience. Asbury's official "Statement of Faith" affirms scripture as the sole basis for the new orthodoxy:

> In the divine inspiration, truthfulness and authority of both the Old and New Testaments, the only written Word of God, without error in all it affirms. The Scriptures are the only infallible rule of faith and practice. The Holy Spirit preserves God's Word in the church today and by it speaks God's truth to peoples of every age;

The Asbury "Ethos Statement" makes explicit the school's anti-gay stand. At the conclusion it reads:

> The Asbury community expects its witness to society today will include personal commitment against prevailing moral laxity by not participating in, advocating, supporting or condoning sexual relationships outside of marriage or homosexual practices, since these are contrary to Scripture and Christian tradition.

When I read this to my ninety-five-year-old mother, a lifelong Methodist churchwoman and Sunday School teacher, she said: "Sanctified ignorance is still ignorance."

The issue of homosexuality came to the fore in the United Methodist Church General Conference in Atlanta in 1972. A friend who was there described how the pernicious language, "homosexuality is incompatible with Christian teaching," made its way into the United Methodist Book of Discipline at that meeting. When the meeting became stalled with invective, a pastor skilled in church politics proposed this language as something on which the majority could agree. When my friend named the delegate responsible for that language, I protested: "But I KNEW him! He was our respected district superintendent in Lubbock when I was in high school." The same churchman, by the way, had declared in 1956 that if Methodist women were ordained to ministry, it would split the church. I learned from my brother John that a good way to know a straight man's attitude toward gays is to observe his views about women.

Abstract and absolutist thought has a long pre-Christian history in Greek philosophy. Like Plato's Ideal Forms, orthodox truths are seen to remain unchanged through time, not subject to imagination or ambiguity. Orthodoxy discounts the power of history and place to revise our understandings of what is true.

I once spent a summer researching texts from Greco-Roman antiquity cited in debates over slavery in the early nineteenth century. Greek and Roman authors were drafted in support of both the pro-slavery and the abolitionist arguments. So too, in about equal measure, were passages from the Bible. A favorite of the pro-slavery side was of course Ephesians 6.5: "Slaves, be obedient to those who are your earthly masters." (RSV)

Sad to say, the publishing arm of the United Methodist Church in 2002 published a book on homosexuality and the Bible with anti-gay readings of selected Biblical texts. I protested to the press representative when I saw the galleys of this book at a meeting of the American Academy of Religion. She explained: "Well, we published a pro-gay book last year."

I refrained from asking her if they also published a pro-slavery book.

MADELEINE L'ENGLE TELLS of how her children's novel *A Wrinkle in Time* routinely makes it onto the list of the ten most frequently-censored books in school and public libraries. She decided one year to read all ten books. She found in common among them this one thing: Imagination.

Imagination is the human gift that enables us to perceive something not yet existing, to work toward ends we may never see. I am fortunate to live in the state that became the thirty-sixth needed to ratify the Women's Suffrage Amendment into the U.S. Constitution in 1920. In hard times, I think of the hundred women and men at the Seneca Falls conference in 1848 who began the long campaign for women's vote. They knew that every single vote at every stage of this struggle would have to be cast by a man. Only one woman at Seneca Falls lived long enough to cast a vote in a presidential election.

Imagination is also the gift that enables us to see more than one side of a question. When we stand on promises, we are standing on the promises of God as we understand them, never on promises we ourselves have defined.

The very faith of Christians rests on an ambiguity: Was Jesus human or divine? The stained-glass windows of Christ Church Cathedral in Nashville were recently taken out to be restored. One of the oldest, "The Ascension Window," had become so begrimed over the decades that the bottom portion was unrecognizable: All one could see was Jesus ascending to Heaven from an opaque blur. When the window came back gleamingly restored, parishioners were astonished to see two footprints left behind on the green grass by the human Jesus as the divine Jesus ascended into heaven.

"Standing" has many connotations: "Here I stand." "Stand by your man." "Stand up and be counted." "Stand up, stand up for Jesus." "Stand and deliver." "What is your standing in this case?" "To stand somewhere, for something." "Standing on the Promises."

To know where we stand in the present requires clarity about our past and imagination about our future. Walter Lippman writes that we must be at peace with the sources of our lives: "If we are ashamed of them, if we are at war with them, they will haunt us forever. They will rob us of our basis of assurance, they will leave us interlopers in the world." Because all institutions are human, they, like all human beings, are flawed. Will Campbell and James Holloway in *Up to Our Steeples in Politics* (1970) are prophetic in reminding us how sinful even the churchly institutions are. Once we recognize our own sins, we become less absolute in judging others as damned or saved.

The ambiguities of faith also require caution about politics and patriotism. The ancient Greeks believed that gods take sides in war. In Homer's *Iliad*, for example, the goddess Athena takes the side of the Greeks, the goddess Aphrodite of the Trojans. I was distressed to hear after September 11 that the Bush Administration was going to root out evil wherever it found it. If none of us is without sin, then rooting out evil will require slicing us all up. The stage for this division of good and evil had been set, of course, by Bush's earlier declaration about the "axis of evil." "Us and them" has become almost acceptable ideology in our current situation, but it remains a heresy going back to the Manichaeans to declare that human beings or nations can be divided into good people and evildoers.

The God of Christians does not take sides. God's promise instead is to stand close by all who suffer. A careful look at Irving Berlin's beloved "God Bless America" can help us here: "Stand beside her and guide her, through the night with a light from above." God is implored to stand by, advise, and guide our actions, not to lead the charge in the service of American interests. A recent documentary about the German theologian Dietrich Bonhoeffer shows chilling footage of swastika flags decking the altars of Christian churches in Germany during the Third Reich as church and uniformed state leaders join hands.

Our human stands, whether we take them in church or in politics or in solemn acts of civil disobedience, are always penultimate. They rest on next-to-last authority. If we consider them ultimate, then we are playing God and Allen Tate is right: We are converting human ideas into abstract absolutes that are the death of religion and of everything else. ■

Ignoring Inequality

Gene Nichol

A COUPLE OF WEEKS before I wrote this essay in the spring of 2004, the U.S. Census Bureau released its most recent study of income and poverty. For the "second consecutive year, the poverty rate and the number living in poverty rose." Almost 35 million Americans (12.1 percent) made less money last year than the extraordinarily modest federal poverty threshold ($18,500 for a family of four). Almost one in five of our children lives in wrenching poverty (compared to one in twelve in most of Europe). The numbers are even worse for black (24 percent) and Hispanic (22 percent) kids. The report could have added that we also apparently lead the world in wealth disparity. The concentration of resources in those at the top of the economic ladder has reached an historic high. The top 10 percent earn 40 percent of our national income. The top 1 percent holds 40 percent of the nation's wealth. Vast privilege has accumulated in the hands of a relative elite that pays itself proportionately more, and pays its workers proportionately less, than the other major industrial democracies.

The story of my own state, North Carolina, was particularly disheartening. Our median family income is now almost $5,000 below the national average. We are one of ten states whose median income actually fell from the year before—in our case by 4.4 percent. About one in seven Tar Heels lives below the poverty line. The Bush Administration says the recession ended in November 2001. You'd have a hard tine proving that in North Carolina.

And more generally, the South has proven to be the native home of American poverty. It continues to sustain the highest poverty rate and the lowest average income of any section of the country. Nearly 14 percent of Southerners are poor and our income levels fall thousands of dollars below national averages. Poverty rates in Louisiana, Arkansas, and Mississippi, for example, lead the nation at almost 20 percent. Yet, ironically, we frequently elect public officials who pander to the wealthy and cripple the social structures available to the poor. Southern leaders often seem to specialize in undermining democracy while giving the back of their hands to meaningful equality. We produce more poverty and more politicians who are untroubled by it than the rest of the nation.

Local newspapers gave the poverty report fairly prominent play. Headlines read: "State's median income dips." But, as usual, it was a one-day story. No expressions of outrage appeared. No emergency proposals followed. The Congress stood mute. The Executive branch was unmoved. No electoral campaigns took up the mantle. Democratic presidential candidates debated the following night without mentioning either the study or poverty. No state legislative initiative was launched. Redistricting and the Ten Commandments continued to hold the floor in our state halls. The story, in the jargon, had no legs. Once each year, whether the economy is booming or sputtering, we learn that the wealthiest nation in human history countenances shockingly high levels of poverty. We discover, yet again, that—despite our vaunted rhetorical

GENE R. NICHOL is Dean of the School of Law and the Burton Craige Professor of Law at the University of North Carolina. Nichol is an author, constitutional lawyer, and civil rights and political activist who hails from Dallas, Texas. He is a regular op-ed columnist for the Raleigh *News & Observer*. He has also written for *The Nation* and other periodicals, as well as most of the country's major law reviews commitment to equality—America accepts more dramatic gaps between the haves and have-nots than the rest of the industrial world. We shrug our shoulders, and we go on.

Income differentials hardly present the whole picture. More than 43 million Americans have no health care. Last year, another 2.5 million lost coverage. In North Carolina, 15.6 percent lack protection. Of households earning under $25,000 a year, about a quarter are uninsured. A third of Hispanics have no health care. The comparison with other industrial nations is particularly galling. We stand alone among the major advanced nations in failing to provide universal coverage—as if we were forced to bolster our economic competitiveness on the backs of the most vulnerable. We spend more per capita on health care than any country in the world. But we also leave more of our fellows in the shadows outside the system. And we do this despite Dr. King's warning that, "of all inequities, inequality in health is the most inhuman."

Economics also drives opportunity. Because schools are financed locally, poverty and inferior education go hand in hand. We countenance rich and poor public schools. Not just private schools, mind you: rich and poor public schools. As if it were thought acceptable to treat some of our children as second- or third-class citizens. In the past three decades, more than forty states have faced serious challenges to unequal public school funding schemes. My own state's *Leandro* decision is not atypical.[1] There, the plaintiffs proved that they were plagued by poor physical facilities, hopelessly outdated book collections, inadequate science labs, nonexistent technology, and inferior teacher salaries. As the Secretary of Housing and Urban Development put it a few years ago, we have moved, again, toward "two educational systems"—one for the children of the wealthy and one for the kids of the poor. Higher education magnifies the inequality. Only 3 percent of the students at the nation's 146 most selective universities come from the bottom economic quartile. An astonishing 74 percent come from the top quarter. Twenty years ago, children from parents in the top quarter were four times more likely to get a college degree than those at the bottom. Now it's ten.[2] America now likely has the most unequal educational system in the industrial world.[3]

With each passing decade, we live in ways that are increasingly polarized along economic lines. More of the poor are consolidated into impoverished neighborhoods—where tensions of crime and social duress multiply. At the same time, increased numbers of the wealthy effectively separate themselves from the rest in exclusive suburbs or gated compounds. Rich and poor share fewer neighborhoods, parks, social services, school districts, local governments, and civic obligations. We occupy divergent communities—separate, non-intersecting spheres. Wealthier citizens have a diminished stake in the quality of life in impoverished neighborhoods. The poor experience the marvels of a consumer-driven, high-technology, information-based economy only through the distant lens of fantastic television programming. Except for the silly lawsuits, it gets harder to remember every year that we are "one nation, under God."

The legal system is perhaps the most inegalitarian of all. Jimmy Carter once claimed that, "ninety percent of our lawyers serve ten percent of our people."[4] That may be an exaggeration. Perhaps. But huge percentages of us are priced out, mystified out, of the voluntary use of the civil justice system. Study after study finds that about 80 percent of the legal need of the poor and near poor goes unmet. Less than one percent of our total national expenditure for lawyers goes toward services for the poor. Legal aid budgets are capped at amounts making effective representation of the poor a statistical impossibility.[5] Even at that, they've been cut by about a third over the last decade. The impoverished are typically left without representation on the most crushing problems of human life—divorce, child custody, domestic violence, housing, and subsistence. But we seem unbothered by the knowledge. We have become coldly accustomed to the idea that it takes six months to try a commercial dispute between powerful corporations and only moments to dispose of an endangered child's abuse and neglect case. We carve "equal justice under law" on our courthouse walls. The sentiment stops there.

Even our political system rewards those who can pay in order to play. Candidates cannot seriously qualify for major political office unless they are wealthy or have access to wealth—in a stunning denial of political equality. The private financing of campaigns systematically skews the outcome of our political processes toward the interests of the economically powerful. Barney Frank told me once that, "we're the only people in the world who insist that our elected officials can walk up to total strangers, ask them for thousands or hundreds of thousands of dollars, get it, and be completely unaffected by it. Achieving a state of perfect ingratitude." Every one of us, of course, knows better. So, the halls of power are increasingly off limits to all but the economically privileged. Those lacking resources fall beyond official purview. And our economic system comes to swamp our political one. A system of government in which those who seek certain policies are allowed to give essentially unlimited amounts of money to those who make the policies may be called many things. But it can't be called democratic. And it can't be called fair.

These fundamental inequities, taken together, reveal that we have succumbed to an increasing and seemingly inexorable trend toward economic apartheid. The stunning disparities in American resources sweep aside our rhetorical claims to equal citizenship. We grant the greatest opportunities to those who are already blessed. We leave standing—unmolested—virtually impenetrable barriers to the progress of the disadvantaged. We refuse to grant many of the core components of human dignity to our fellows that other nations provide without debilitation. We offer only a feigned justice, while celebrating a supposed foundational commitment to legal equity. Dramatic economic polarization damages our possibilities of common venture. Separation impairs our ability to see each other as peers. The skills and sustenance necessary to assure meaningful political participation are ignored. As Franklin Roosevelt put it, "necessitous men are not free men."[6] The ideal of equal citizenship is effectively removed from our public lives. Across a broad array of enterprises, we have allowed the deck to become stacked against those lodged at the bottom.

And we know it.

Yet decade after decade, in cultural arena after cultural arena, in election after election, these crushing problems are barely discussed. In law, in politics, in philosophy, in letters, we simply turn our gaze away. Barbara Ehrenreich has written, correctly, that "the poor have disappeared from the culture at large, from its political rhetoric, its intellectual endeavors, from its daily entertainment." In American life, formal equality has become submerged in a torrent of disadvantage. Lincoln thought that the "central idea of America" was that the weak would gradually be made stronger and ultimately all would have an equal chance. Barbara Jordan put it similarly: "government has an obligation to actively seek to remove those obstacles that block individual achievement—obstacles emanating from race, sex and economic condition." That obligation is "indigenous to the American ideal." But what was "central" for Lincoln and "indigenous" to Jordan is alien to us. We have come to think that a regime of economic apartheid is unremarkable, unavoidable, and untroubling.

Of course, until fifty years ago, we regarded a debilitating and brutal framework of racial apartheid as "natural" and beyond disturbance. It, too, was an unavoidable "private" ordering—not the appropriate concern of our courts or constitutions. Chief Justice

Earl Warren's opinion in *Brown v. Board of Education,* however, pulled away layers of rationalization and silent embrace of atrocity. Warren concluded that the lessons of history and text that had provided endless bases for constitutional dispute "cast some light, [but they are] not enough to resolve the problem with which we are faced." Whether or not integration of the public schools was contemplated by the framers of the fourteenth amendment, by 1954, education had become "the most important function of state and local governments." It is "required in the performance of our most basic responsibilities, . . . it is the foundation of good citizenship." It is the "principal instrument in awakening the child to cultural values." "In these days," Warren concluded, "it is doubtful that any child may reasonably be expected to succeed in life if he is denied the opportunity" of an equal education.

Warren came close to saying, simply, that if the practices challenged in *Brown* could stand unmolested by America's constitutional notions of equality, then American concepts of equality aren't worth much. To the same end, if the fourteenth amendment's equal protection clause is fundamentally agnostic about literally and systematically debilitating differences in condition, it's not worth much either. Of course, constitutional intervention would require a theory of judicial power that is at least congenial to the belief that heightened judicial obligations arise in circumstances of clear democratic failure. In the past two decades, our federal courts have more typically been the friends of the powerful and privileged than of the dispossessed. But if courts are to thwart legislative directives—if the power of judicial review is to be comprehensible in a democracy committed to majority rule—it makes sense to focus attentions on systematic exclusion from political opportunity. And the more our economic system dominates our political one, the greater the argument necessarily becomes for judicial efforts to tackle issues of economic justice.

Moving economic inequality and privation to the national agenda would also require a politics of vibrancy and ambition. It would demand an understanding that our virtue as a nation is still in the making; that, no less than our predecessors, we are charged to make the promises of democracy real. It would demand a recognition that our system of individual freedom sometimes results in morally unacceptable concentrations of wealth and resources. It would be rooted in an insistence that our governments should not operate as mere executive committees of the powerful and the privileged; that segregation and polarization impair our ability to see each other as peers. It would remind us that the most powerful American value is that we're all in this together; that we are, in fact, committed to liberty and justice for all. It would require that we be realistic enough to concede that actual political equality demands attention to the skills and sustenance necessary for meaningful participation. It would reflect an embrace of constitutional democracy's call to a continuing reformist struggle to protect the weak from the strong. Most importantly, it would return to the center of our political agenda the largest problems that we face as a nation.

A couple of months ago, I read Ralph Ellison's posthumously published novel *Juneteenth*. There, Ellison's main character says this:

> "We are a nation born in blood, fire and sacrifice. Thus we are judged, questioned, weighed—by the ideals and events which marked [our] founding. These transcendent ideals interrogate us, judge us, pursue us, in . . . what we do, or do not do. They accuse us ceaselessly, and their interrogation is ruthless, scathing . . . until, reminded of who we are, and what we are about, and the cost[s] we have assumed, we pull ourselves together. We lift our eyes to the hills and we arise."

Our constitutive calls to equal dignity, opportunity and justice surely interrogate and accuse us. They judge us and find us lacking. The answers we offer and the excuses we provide do not satisfy. Not if we are what we claim to be.

Bernard Bailyn has argued that the central theme of revolutionary American ideology was "the belief that through the ages it has been privilege—artificial, man-made, man-secured privilege—ascribed to some, denied to others that has crushed men's hopes of fulfillment."[7] But the embrace of privilege in modern American life has become not only pervasive; it is now almost second nature, an acquired and unexamined skin. And what, we might further ask, is the "central theme" of modern American political thought? Does it include any actual, life-charging commitment to equality? Is it, in any non-farcical sense, rooted in the rhetorical notion that we are all in this together? One nation, indivisible? The growing, silent marriage of privilege and privation mocks the American commitment to constitutional democracy. We ignore it at the cost of our national mission. We look past it at the cost of our best selves. ■

My Yellow Ribbon Town: A Meditation on My Country and My Home

Paul M. Gaston

At the outset of my country's "shock and awe" adventurism, I was persuaded that it was both unjustified and potentially disastrous. When Nelson Mandela singled out the United States as a major threat to world peace, I feared for more than our standing in the community of nations. When an acquaintance close to the inner circle of decision makers told me that Iraq was but one of several countries the Administration might have chosen to attack and that the "war on terrorism" would likely involve military action against any Muslim countries that might become supply stations for our terrorist enemies, I knew my fears were justified.

What I believed to be true in the spring of 2003 gradually came to be widely acknowledged. By November, intelligence expert Thomas Powers summed up what virtually everyone outside the Bush-Cheney-Rice-Rumsfeld-Wolfowitz sphere of influence would admit: "On the eve of war, and probably for years beforehand," he wrote, "Iraq had no weapons of mass destruction and it had no active program to build them." The justification for the war "was not merely flawed or imperfect—it was wrong in almost every detail, and completely wrong at the heart. There was no imminent danger—indeed there was no *distant* danger. Saddam Hussein had no weapons of mass destruction to give to al-Qaeda or anyone else."[1]

No president in our history has been the object of such worldwide anathema as George W. Bush. Never has American foreign policy been so devastatingly dissected by the international press. Never have so many millions of citizens around the world gathered to protest what they call our march to empire. Government spokesmen and their media allies dismiss the criticism as jealousy-inspired anti-Americanism. Which it is not. The Indian novelist Arundhati Roy, among the most eloquent of our foreign critics, pays homage to America's "rich tradition of resistance" and credits today's Americans with being among the most insightful opponents of their nation's policies. History, she says, is giving American dissenters the chance to make their country into something it should be, but is not—a great nation, true to its highest ideals.[2]

SOON AFTER THE BUSH REGIME sent its armed forces into Iraq, wondering like so many others what I could possibly say or do that might make a difference, I set off for my home state of Alabama. My first stop was Monroeville, where the Alabama Writers Forum was holding its annual meeting. I had been invited to talk on a recently published book in which I wrote about the American conviction of our moral and physical impregnability, the myths we held to of our innocence and invincibility.[3] What I had to say was not new, but I thought it was timely.

With varying emphases throughout their history, Americans have stressed the belief that theirs is an exceptional nation, different from and superior to those of the rest of the world. Its ideology of freedom and equality set it above the Old World's heritage of feudalism and privilege. With the end of the Cold War it stood like a colossus ready to spread its claimed virtues, the world's only superpower and best democracy, innocent and invincible. After the September 11 attacks the Bush regime called on these beliefs shamelessly. When it decided to launch its revolutionary preemptive strike against Iraq it raised them as shields against truths about both past and present.

Monroeville was a good place to be. Those who write and read honest books, I reasoned, should be the vanguard of the movement to unmask falsehoods and reveal the motivations underlying them. I was not disappointed by the people I met there. They were a receptive and lively group of authors, young and old, novices and old hands, poets and novelists and nonfiction writers of all sorts. It was energizing to be in their company. All of them—or at least all I heard or spoke to—shared, in one degree or another, my anxieties and warmly endorsed what I had to say about the misleading myths of innocence and invincibility. Like me, they hoped to find a way to stand against the peril to which the Bush regime seemed to be leading us; but, also like me—though they would speak of the power of the written word—they were not sure that what we wrote might make a difference. Writing, however, was our calling. It was what we could do.

MY NEXT STOP WAS FAIRHOPE, home of the unique utopian community on the shores of Mobile Bay. My grandfather, who was its founder and guiding force for more than forty years, was himself a fine writer, a newspaper editor and pamphleteer of rare distinc-

PAUL M. GASTON, Professor Emeritus of Southern and Civil Rights History at the University of Virginia, was born and reared in the Fairhope, Alabama, Single Tax Colony. A past president of the Southern Regional Council, he is the Lillian Smith Award-winning author of *The New South Creed*, of two books on the Fairhope colony, and of numerous pamphlets and articles on racial matters.

tion. But he placed his hopes for reform elsewhere. He wrote that "they that shall make good theories work and prove the value of proposed social solutions by practical demonstration will do far more to move the world than the wisest and most brilliant theorists."[4] His life work was to try to do precisely that, "to prove the value of proposed social solutions by practical demonstration."

As I drove down the black ribbon of highway knifing through familiar red clay banks edging pine forests, my imagination ran back to the fall of 1894 when my grandfather and grandmother, along with their four children, the youngest still in diapers, traveled through the forebears of these same woods as passengers on the Mobile & Ohio Railroad headed for what they had come to call their "promised land." Their fair hopes for creating a city on a hill must have been tried as they neared their destination, which they would find to be a desolate, thickly wooded site high on a bluff on the eastern shore of Mobile Bay. Nothing on the route they were traveling could have been familiar to them. How could they not have experienced at least a little anxiety? Family lore, however, has it that my grandfather, just turned thirty-three, was unshakably optimistic, filled with confidence in his ability to create a model community free from the gross exploitation, inequality, and manifold injustices of Gilded Age America. He thought they were realistic when they named their soon-to-be-founded community Fairhope.

Now I was driving toward the town he had created and directed for forty years and which my father had led for thirty-six more after him. Fairhope was my spiritual home, the place where my values were shaped and my moral compass established. I looked forward to roaming the bluffs above the Bay and the beaches along the shore, and to reflecting once again on the dreams that had been woven into the place of my birth and rearing. I longed for a time machine to transport me to that train, carrying my grandfather along to his destination. We would talk about what he really expected to accomplish and why he had risked so much against such formidable odds.

As I reflected on what he had written about the imperfections and injustices of his America, and on the better world he hoped to create, the dark thoughts I had about my country, now more than a century later, kept intruding. I remembered a passage from one of his early writings in which he lamented that it was impossible to live in his America without becoming enmeshed in one form or another of exploitation or injustice and the abandonment of principle. The pressure merely to exist, he wrote, moved even a good man to turn "his back on what he knows to be his true self and higher convictions [and] to pursue with the utmost concentration of his energies the prize of material gain."[5] It was a world he could no longer abide. As I ticked off a partial list of parallels in my own life, I wondered how much longer I could abide them. Lacking his vigor and courage I reckoned I would do little more than list them:

- The cable that speeded up my internet connection and gave me too many television channels was provided by Adelphia, its founders shown on the evening news carried off to jail for their thievery;

- HealthSouth, the rehabilitation hospital where good women and men helped me recover from a knee-replacement operation, was owned by another set of thieves, with headquarters in Alabama, of all places;

- My telephone service once came from MCI, a division of WorldCom; its executives stole millions and wondered why anyone would want them to grace the presence of our prison system (a fate the worst of them continue to evade);

- My electric power was never routed by Enron, but I knew many who relied on it and I grieved for the employees sent into poverty and despair by the thievery of its executives;

- I never had the need for an accountant, but kinspersons had once worked for Arthur Anderson, chief facilitating servant of the corporate crooks;

- Family members and friends shopped at Wal-Mart, chief exemplar of the right to pay poverty wages and to abuse workers;

- My own university rivaled Wal-Mart, housing its well-paid guests in motels that refused to pay a living wage. And why not? Hiding behind the mantra of privatization it allowed the payment of poverty wages to hundreds of the workers who sustained its daily existence.

Like my grandfather, I saw these and other crimes of my day as consequences of the structure of our society and the values that shaped and maintained it, not the aberrant wanderings of a few errant individuals. They reached so far into every aspect of our daily lives that only a hermit living off nuts and berries in the forest could escape their tentacles. They were so common and omnipresent, almost like the air we breathed, that our lives became inured to them. I thought of the chocolate I was munching as I drove, knowing that the beans from which it was made were harvested by child slave labor. And what of the coffee I had drunk with my breakfast in Monroeville? What exploited workers had plucked its beans?

All these somber thoughts, ricocheting off my meditation with my grandfather, deepened my dismay over the support with which my fellow citizens sustained our president. In the midst of war his regime was mobilized to impose on our conquered lands the very values I was lamenting, all with minimal opposition from a morally benumbed citizenry. The democracy of which the administration spoke so glibly was married to an aggressive brand of "free market capitalism" that not only permitted but encouraged this very undermining of democratic values. At home, the economic policies it favored—from benefit-the-rich tax reform to the evisceration of Medicare—came wrapped in an ideology my grandfather would have called "unnatural and unjust" because it violated the "natural rights" of its citizens, and was "at war with the nobler impulses of humanity, and opposed to its highest development."

In his call to fellow reformers to join him in creating an alternative, model community, he wrote that "the present social and economic order is doomed. In the height of its marvelous achievements it bears within itself the seeds of its own destruction. Clearheaded economists and warmhearted philanthropists long ago pointed out and denounced its enormous waste of human energy and natural resources and its hideous injustice and cruelty." Of reformers like himself, he wrote, "the injustice and attendant want, misery, hardships and despair everywhere apparent fill his life with sadness."[6] I knew what he meant, what he felt.

FAIRHOPE WAS, literally, a city on a hill. Captivated by the beauty of the site, my grandfather wrote lyrically about his first view of it:

> Here we have a short strip of sandy beach, then a narrow park ranging in width from 100 to 250 feet and covered with almost every variety of shrub and tree which flourishes in this locality—pine, live oak, magnolia, cedar, juniper, cypress, gum, holly, bay, beech, youpon and myrtle. On the east side of this "lower park," as we call it, a red clay bluff rises up almost perpendicularly to a height of nearly 40 feet. Along its serried edge tall, arrowy pines

stand like sentinels looking out to sea.[7]

Those sentinels stood guard over the creation of what the Fairhopers designed to be a demonstration of what they called "cooperative individualism," a guide to a fulfilling life free of the extremes of poverty and wealth, exploitation and unchecked individualism, so tightly woven into the America they were hoping to reform. Their struggle to achieve these goals went on year after year, often with what appeared to be no hope of success, but they persisted. By the 1920s, the model community cast a small beam of idealism and hope, providing land and opportunity for men and women of modest means and winning accolades from visiting northern writers and reformers.

For a boy growing up in the Fairhope of the 1930s and '40s, as I did, the fair hopes of 1894 seemed everywhere to have been fulfilled. What such a youngster experienced most immediately in those years was a sense of freedom and security in an environment of harmony and sensuous beauty. The settlement spread back from the water's edge, just as my grandfather had first described it, making its way from the shoreline up the cliffs to the gently rising table land at their summit. In retrospect, I think of it as a nurturing communal park. There were no private homes or commercial structures monopolizing either views or access to the Bay. In addition to the Bay, the sandy beaches, and the wooded bluffs, there were ravines with red-clay banks and white-sand bottoms that cut through the town; and, not far away, a deep, clear, cold, freshwater creek, overhung with oak limbs festooned with Spanish moss. These natural treasures were our Shangri-La. Nowhere did we see "private property" or "keep out" signs. Nor was there a big house on a hill or a rich planter or banker to stand over us. The community's special treasures belonged to us all, shielded against the ravages of wealth, power, and privilege.

Inspired by Henry George's belief in land as our common inheritance and his tempered version of the cooperative commonwealth, the Fairhopers joined to their radical economic and social practices equally radical educational ideas. In our "organic" school, as we called it—attending to the whole person, body, mind, and spirit—we found another place of security and freedom. With our broad academic curriculum joined with art, crafts, dance, drama, and music classes, we grew up feeling the school was for us, not that we were to fit into some preconceived notion of what we ought to be or become. The absence of grades, honors, rewards, punishments, and failure in an atmosphere where we and our ideas were at the center of things was something we found stimulating and supportive. We came to learn because we wanted to. We also internalized a lived experience of democracy and equality in ways no civics lesson or history class could teach.[8]

Somewhere along the way, still a young boy, I learned that all these blessings were neither accidental nor the natural order of things in the United States, much less in the American South. I have strong memories of my father reading to me the constitution of our community, written by his father, declaring that Fairhope was to be "a model community . . . free from all forms of private monopoly" where its citizens would have "equality of opportunity, the full reward of individual effort and the benefits of cooperation in matters of general concern." On other occasions, my father read to me his father's declaration that Fairhope was designed "to establish justice, to remove the opportunities for the preying of one upon another." In one of his letters he wrote: "We close the gates against injustice; we open them to unselfishness. Society can do no more." These and other colony aphorisms became part of my early learning and consciousness so that I came to feel that we not only had an obligation to struggle for justice but that we were armed with special insights into how it could be achieved.

Our lives seemed to be lived with high purpose.[9]

As I turned off the interstate onto the commercially blighted last stretch of highway into Fairhope, dark broodings crowded out my reverie. Musings on the colony's idealistic origins and inspiring early history gave way to melancholy. I felt a sharp sense of loss over the faded sense of a life once lived with high purpose; the subversion of a reformist mission; and the end of free land that had been Fairhope's *raison d'être*, its road to the realization of the fair hopes of ordinary Americans. At the Monroeville meeting one of the writers, a Fairhoper who lived out in the country, closed the inscription of her new book to me with the rueful truth that she was "too po' to live in the single tax colony."

Unknowingly, I suspect, what she wrote was a bitter epitaph for my grandfather's dream and my father's life work. Quite apart from all of Fairhope's many charms and attractions—the beauty of the bay, gullies, pine forests, and tree-lined streets; the vitality of its writers and artists; the visits of the John Deweys, Clarence Darrows, and Upton Sinclairs; the uniqueness and fame of the school; the binding experience of democratic communalism—the colony's fundamental distinguishing feature, the one from which all else derived, was its land policy. Modifying Henry George's single tax theory, the colony owned, and made freely available to its lessees, land which it rented for homes, businesses, and farms. In exchange for the rental payment, the colony paid all taxes levied on the land and improvement of its lessees—a simulated version of George's single tax on land values. Two generations and more of settlers, most of them men and women of modest means, attributed their material security and sense of personal worth to the free land that gave them their start, all in a culture where land speculation and exploitation were shared anathema.

If my writer friend's inscription provided Fairhope's epitaph, the spirited woman who cut my hair pronounced its consequences. I came to her shop (she would never have called it a salon) soon after my arrival and almost immediately she began dissecting contemporary Fairhope. She never goes down the picturesque main street, she told me, because "they have too many rich people there building condos they won't even live in." Fairhope, she informed me, "has become a place for rich people." With a sardonic edge in her voice she told me how the previous mayor had gone on a visit to Carmel, California, to come back with a scheme for turning Fairhope into the Carmel on the Bay. Now, she said, it was filled with all those silly boutiques. Why, she wanted to know, "would anyone spend $500 on a pair of shoes." She didn't mention it, but I couldn't help thinking of one of the new shops for upscale ladies apparel I had seen on my early morning walk. It was called, without irony, Utopia.

Having no idea who I was (or who my father and grandfather had been) my haircutter's mood expanded. It was plain wrong, she said, for people to be spending all that money, tearing down houses and buildings all over the town to replace them with huge expensive ones; it was plain wrong to be spending all that money "when there are people homeless, people in the streets, people in poverty." Right on, I said silently, wanting to tell her that she was an authentic Fairhoper. Then, turning mellow for a moment, she told me she had once seen a picture book history of Fairhope. It seemed to her that not only had life been simpler then; it had been better. People got along, enjoyed what they had, lived a good life without "all this showing off, this pretension, this looking down on you." Then her *coup de grâce*: "People like me had a chance back then."

AFTER MY HAIRCUT I took a long walk through my old neighborhood, the area now called "the historic district." A block up from the bay, in front of the home where my mother and her family first lived, and across the street from the park where my father had proposed to her, I exchanged the morning greeting with a fashionably dressed young woman out on a stroll with her dog. We fell into pleasant conversation. Her face lit up with pleasure when I asked her if she liked living in Fairhope. "Oh, yes, indeed," she replied, explaining that she and her husband had moved there just a few years previous, choosing it because, well, because of its beauty, its charming boutiques, and good restaurants. The people were all friendly and, well, she gave a sigh of satisfaction, "it is safe." I recalled, but did not mention, *Safe Places East*, a book for retirement-seekers. Fairhope is the only Alabama community it features.[10]

Unspoken in this encounter or in Fairhope booster literature is the enforced whiteness of the town. Almost immediately on their arrival, the founders made a fateful decision to restrict their model community to white people, but they did so in the full knowledge that they were violating the fundamental principle they had set out to demonstrate. When a supporter of the colony raised questions about the exclusion policy, there was no evasion in my grandfather's reply. "The criticism of our friend," he wrote, "illustrates anew the difficulties and differences of opinion arising in the effort to determine how far we can practically go in the 'application of correct theories' within a general condition of applied incorrect ones over which we have no control." Racial discrimination, he agreed, was wrong: "We believe in 'universal equality'—equality of rights"; no man had "more moral or natural right to any particular portion of the earth, the common heritage of mankind, than any other of his fellow men." But when he asked if the colony should "follow the naked principle of equality unreservedly, regardless of existing conditions" he could not advise it. To do so, he believed, would stir the wrath of the neighboring white Southerners and bring to a cruel end the infant experiment.[11]

In the decades that followed, the "existing conditions" that had occasioned the exclusion policy in the first place did not ease. Both my grandfather and my father spoke and wrote against the white supremacy culture, but could not lead the colony or the town government to abandon its commitment to segregation. In fact, as the years wore on and new generations were born into and grew up in a world of segregation, many of the singletaxers came to believe that there was no conflict between the principles of their demonstration and the continuation of a whites-only policy. By the 1960s one of the most prominent among them was a George Wallace ally, and others fell easily in line behind Alabama's most influential white supremacist.

Fairhope's population swelled with newcomers in the last decades of the twentieth century. Few of them knew of or identified with the founding mission. At the same time, the Single Tax Corporation played an ever-diminishing role in the life of the town. Its landholdings had not increased significantly for decades, the town government owned and maintained the public utilities once identified with the colony, and the rising popularity of the entire eastern shore drove land values up sharply. The Corporation, unable to diminish land speculation, acquiesced in the transfers of its most desirable lands for huge sums of money. In the midst of all these boom times the town annexed areas to the north, where well-to-do whites lived, but firmly resisted vigorous demands from black leaders to annex contiguous areas to the south, where they lived. The "existing conditions" of the 1890s and 1960s had vanished, but racial mores were now too deeply entrenched—and too little challenged—to permit a reckoning with history and a righting of wrongs. Fairhope became, almost as never before, an enclave of white people, of, increasingly, well-to-do white people.

I continued my walk in silence. Everywhere there was evidence of my haircutter's complaint. Charming homes, authentic reminders of the egalitarian roots of the model community, were crumbling before the bulldozer, making way for the mansions of the rich that so aroused the ire of the few remaining Fairhopers.

Then there were the yellow ribbons. Hardly a yard was without one, tied to a post box, fixed to a tree, laced in a doorway, all shown off by the manicured lawns they graced. Their message was reinforced along the way by "support our troops" signs. "Stand up for peace" placards were nowhere to be seen. Yellow ribbons, manicured lawns, and giant new homes—this was the Fairhope of the twenty-first century.

The new Organic School building, too, was festooned with ribbons, but at least it had not followed the lead of the intermediate school where the pupils had successfully demanded that the luncheon menu identify the fried potatoes as "freedom fries." I suppose eleven- and twelve-year-olds, inspired by what they heard at home, could earn one's empathy. When the Congress of the United States similarly changed its menu I decided against calling the action childish. That would have been to deliver an insult to children. I settled for petulant.

This lockstep display of ribbons and signs, as I was to learn later, came in part at the request of the mayor. Fairhope, he apparently believed, should have its patriotism mobilized and on display. I had once been one of "our troops"—a squad leader in a mortar section of a weapons platoon of an Army infantry company. I wore my uniform proudly and felt admired in it, both at home and overseas. But the thought that I and my comrades were being used for a cause that was less than noble never crossed the minds of anyone I knew or had ever heard of. Now, in 2003, the young men and women who wanted to be proud and admired in the uniforms they wore had to wonder. Why had their government scorned the United Nations? Why had it driven their historic allies from their side? Why were they in this war and its aftermath with so little world support? Why was the outcome so uncertain? These questions would come to haunt more of them in the months ahead.

I was joined for lunch that day by one of the old Fairhopers, a woman absorbed with organizing a tour of "historic" homes ("see them before they are torn down"), writing vignettes of Fairhope's golden days, and still struggling to bring the Organic School back to its founding principles. As we reflected on the yellow ribbons and the disappearing homes she recounted the story of a Single Tax stalwart who had told an Elderhostel class that if E. B. Gaston were to walk the streets of Fairhope today he would know that the model community of his dreams had become a reality. We both shook our heads in disbelief, not needing to say that it would be my grandfather's nightmare, not his dream, that he would encounter.

The parading of nightmares as dreams come true had begun well before the Elderhostel lecture. More than a decade earlier, the then mayor, returning from a European trip that filled him with a new vision of Fairhope's future, said that he had "a burning desire to make Fairhope the most beautiful, charming city that you could find anywhere in this country."[12] Beauty and charm. E. B. Gaston had no objection to either; indeed, early Fairhopers created the parks, protecting them in perpetuity from private and profiteering enterprise, and lined the avenues with the magnolias and oaks that gave it the beauty so enticing to the newcomers. But where was the mayor's "burning desire" for free land, for "a model community . . . free from all forms of private monopoly" where its citizens would have "equality of opportunity, the full reward of individual effort and the benefits of co-operation in matters of general concern." There was no such desire, burning or otherwise. But the author of the popular pictorial history could write that, because of this mayor's vision and leadership, the "tradition of 'cooperative individualism' is alive and well among us one hundred years after Gaston coined the phrase."[13]

I LEFT FAIRHOPE UNSURE of what my days there had taught me about the state of our union. Three out of four Fairhope voters opted for George W. Bush in 2000. By the twenty-first century the South had become the engine driving the Republican Party. The story of how this had come about is complicated, but we know it was anchored in the race-based "southern strategy" Nixon launched at the end of the 1960s and the "social issues" strategy his successors added a quarter-century later. The first brought well-to-do whites into the party; the second wooed those at the lower end of the income scale. But Fairhope? Even in conservative Alabama its 75 percent vote for Bush was nineteen points higher than the state total of 56 percent.

What seemed to stand out most clearly for me in Fairhope's history was the gradual erosion of the options open to the colony leaders, the inevitable declining significance of its land policy, and then the dissipation of the idealism and vision of most of its remaining members and leaders. All of this made it easy for the molders of the new Fairhope to appropriate the luster and beauty of the historic community and to convert it into a fortified jewel of contented conservatism. We historians write about unintended consequences. I cannot imagine a better example than what I saw in the walks I took through my hometown in the spring of 2003. I know my father and grandfather would have felt the same way.

Fortified jewels of contented conservatism exist all over America, of course, more of them in the South than ever before. Flying their yellow ribbons, they have cut themselves off from the historic roots of American idealism and are the backbone of the Bush regime. They will mobilize to thwart regime change in 2004. We who will strive to prevail against them need to keep alive our fair hopes that the call for a revival of America's "rich tradition of resistance" will be answered. It will be a resistance faithful to the dream of a more worthy America, perhaps with the power of recapturing those who have abandoned it.

For Fairhope it is probably too late to change significantly the voting percentages in 2004, but it is not too late for a once energizing tradition of resistance to be revitalized. I have written in this essay about the spirit of the woman who cut my hair, but not of the band of writers, artists, and free thinkers that still distinguishes Fairhope from other non-university Southern communities. They once set the tone of the model community; they are now an embattled minority. On my last visit one of them showed me a book my grandfather had inscribed to her. "Yours for justice," he had written in his bold hand. "Why don't we stand up for justice again?" my friend asked me. It was a good question. ■

Our Imperiled Union

Leslie Dunbar

I SAY IMPERILED not from apprehension of an external threat, or even overt repudiation of the Constitution, but from belief that the Bush II Administration, in succession of others dating back to the war against the Vietnamese, yet outreaching all, is embedding in our polity principles transformative of the republic.

One of life's facts I have to cope with is that there are citizens—millions of them!—who think differently than I about George W. Bush and his administration. The record seems to me, and to the political multitude of which I am part, so overwhelmingly clear that that support is baffling. But there it is.

This is indeed a divided nation. Mr. Bush once, in the foggy past of his national rise, asserted that he was an uniter, not a divider. If he believed that at all, he must have meant that people would rally to his flag, once raised; that he and his politics would become the national will.

For a while, in the post-9/11 and early prewar months, it appeared this might be so, as a public which perceived itself under foreign attack instinctively sought unity. But even before September 11, 2001, and despite the questionable legitimacy of his presidency, Mr. Bush had acted as if he were the nation's mandated leader, and a nerveless Democratic party allowed that. The Democrats' crushing defeat in the congressional elections of

2002 almost was a coronation. But times have changed.

In this era when wealth leads and regularly controls politicians of both parties it is easy to be cynical—not merely complaining or dissenting—about American politics, and anxiously troubled and angry over its directions. When this old patriot that I am reads the daily news, he looks for but finds little or no reported effort of this president and his administration to curb the greed of wealthy interests that is manuring the dirt from which this pervasive cynicism roots itself and flourishes. They seem, on the contrary, the antagonist of any viable concept of common interest or good.

The Constitution announces as one of its grand principles, indeed the first of all, the forming of "a more perfect union." I see that union as being one where all citizens would have realistic chances for a good and satisfying life; where there is one and the same law for all; where all including the government obey it; and where no high and rigid barriers separate us from each other.

The South has twice sought to shatter the union, first and most tragically by secession and civil war, and then in our own time by its shameless defiance of court-ordered school desegregation. One might think George W. Bush, widely and accurately accepted as a Southerner, ought to be therefore acutely sensitive

---

Leslie W. Dunbar, a native of West Virginia, was executive director of the Southern Regional Council during the turmoil of the 1960s, and has been closely involved with the cause of Southern democracy since. He directed the Field Foundation and oversaw its commitment, in the 1960s and '70s, to child welfare and civil rights. He is most recently the author of *The Shame of Southern Politics*. He now lives in Washington, D.C.

to the needs of national unity. He has not been. If he and his administration are much longer in office, the economic interests they respond to in Pavlovian predictability much longer ascendant, the essentials of unity will be under heavy stress. And again from a Southern-led party.

The South retreated from the recklessness of the post-*Brown* period by reacquainting itself with the political imperatives of moderation. It had to learn and accept that fairness is basic to the orderly governance of a democratic polity; that political leadership in a democracy requires and depends upon respect for law; and that people's lives are stultified by a politics that is based on ideology, on dogma that declares there is an overriding creed before which all policies must yield.

Once and for long in the South that dominating creed was white supremacy. To call upon it could render impotent any reasoned dissent. In the same way today the Bush Administration would scare off all questioning by invoking "national security." How often does Mr. Bush say that his responsibility is to protect us, to make us safe, or words to that effect! And derivative of security—or companion to it—is "our" free and competitive economic system.

The South once learned enough of the truths of moderation that in the knowing of them it could make itself into a region where people have a probable chance of living in peace and prosperity with each other.

A liberal's thoughts about Mr. Bush and his Southern-inspired national party may shift only within a narrow range, depending on the news of the day and one's varying temper. Anger, disgust, outrage are nearly always at hand; sometimes one may be incredulous, appalled, or feel embattled.

But always, I worry. Those other moods are not to be denied, but worry over what the presidency of George W. Bush means to our (and to lands beyond) present and future is the main concern.

Today's South and the Republican Party, of which it has become the present dynamo, need to learn and know that "a more perfect union" is not a matter of victory over one's opponents—not a game of "in your face" judicial appointments, to give one example—but a result of statecraft requiring those same three political values that the South had to learn in the turmoil over civil rights: *fairness; respect for the rule of law; and the shunning of ideology.* Those principles have been unlearned by the present Southern-led Republican Party.

After the Republicans rammed to passage the Medicare bill of November 2003, which the usually friendly *Washington Post* called "government by juggernaut" and of which Mr. Norman Ornstein of the conservative American Enterprise Institute was moved to write that "the ugliness of this one will linger," the astute and fair-minded David Broder wrote, "Narrowly based actions by all branches of government add fuel to the fires of division. It is easy—temptingly easy—to say that those in power should exercise restraint rather than force through large actions on the basis of narrow—or nonexistent—majorities."

FAIRNESS. Was this also a recrudescence of the "massive resistance" South of the post-1954 days, of that white Southern political culture which was uncomfortable with, intolerant of, dissent within its ranks? Did it manifest an even more historic Southern trait, one that W. J. Cash and other interpreters have described: a deep-seated demand for regional conformity? At any rate, Southern Republicans seem to come by it naturally. The Republicans' party discipline is astounding (in some state legislatures of the present-day South as well).

2003 saw the retirement from the U.S. Senate of the last of those ideologically crazed leaders of the mid-century "massive resistance": Strom Thurmond of South Carolina. He had long ago passed into a quiet servanthood of avarice and of acquiescence in party priorities. He was shortly followed out by North Carolina's fanatical and domineering Jesse Helms. Their exits changed nothing except a possible enhancement of the party's energy from younger replacements. The weight of the South's congressional strength will still, unless bold new spirits emerge from the region, tilt toward the rich and away from the poor, even away from the non-rich middle class.

But so does that of the whole Congress, and for Mr. Bush and his administration it is not a tilt but crushing power. This is, as that latter-day hero Senator Robert Byrd of West Virginia has said, a government of the wealthy, by the wealthy, for the wealthy. Crudely it often claims to act in the interests of the poor and non-rich, if only they will but patiently wait and see.

To point this out, as a growing number of commentators and politicians are doing, is to be accused of "class warfare." It is an ignorant charge (for the only coherent economic class as yet in our nation is the corporate rich). But why demur? Some revolt of the lower ranks of the American economy might be all to the good. By 2000, our CEOs' compensation was reportedly *1,531 times* that of hourly workers; the differential grows until death and even beyond through the astounding disparity of retirement benefits.[1]

Other essays in this book describe the disparities more adequately. Surely, our *union* cannot indefinitely hold in an environment of such inequality; quite possibly no society's unity could. Nor can what tenuous quietude that now exists among the world's poor be expected indefinitely to endure it.

The infamous "robber barons" of our past got their wealth mainly through acquiring capital, often ruthlessly. Our present "class" of oligarchs mostly enrich themselves as managers of other people's assets, other people's money. Mr. Bush's administration's domestic program is founded on tax cuts. Such is their solution for just about everything. They make out "taxes" to be a bad thing *per se*, virtually un-American unless for "national security" (and even for that they prefer to borrow).

Others can debate the economic wisdom of this policy. Even if that were held to be positive, it is cruelly harsh toward the poor among us, who have their rightful place in the social compact. The incontrovertible fact is that for some considerable period of time the Republican tax cuts reduce the government's ability to aid the non-rich or to lessen the vast disparities of benefits that now derive not from personal accomplishment or merit, but from simply being part of American society.

Adam Smith, although certainly no enthusiast for "taking from the pockets of the people," gave over many pages of his *The Wealth of Nations* to discussing the numerous kinds of taxes and their various effects, and laid down as a first principle, "The subjects of every state ought to contribute towards the support of the government, as nearly as possible, in proportion to their respective abilities; that is, in proportion to the revenue which they respectively enjoy under the protection of the state.—In the observation or neglect of this maxim consists, what is called the equality or inequality of taxation."[2] Justice Oliver Wendell Holmes, Jr., was right that taxes are the price paid for civilization. They make possible any society. They also lessen the debt we ask later generations to pay. The Republicans of this administration and Congress seem, however, to regard that as of no matter, in obsessive insistence that minimal taxation of the wealthy will profit the nation for all foreseeable time.

Taxes also make possible, and Republicans see this perhaps the most clearly, a modest redistribution of wealth toward the interests and needs of the non-rich, and toward the common good. They make possible investment in schools, public health, and for a host of other present shortcomings of the nation's social structure: in many ways, we have a mission of "nation building" to do here, within our own shores.

Moreover, what other realistic way is there in twenty-first century America, for creating job opportunities for all, in an economy that has demonstrated to any who look without ideological blinkers that—short of an all-out foreign war—its productivity has little need for everybody. The Bush party, in ideological campaigns for "privatizing," is destructive of the present well-being of many, of persons who in a thoroughly "privatized," Darwinian economy would be the weakest of the weak. In time, economists will have to recognize that there is such a thing as technological unemployment, that structural mal-distribution of wealth and income is unavoidable in capitalism. And that, therefore, a government intent on serving all its citizens, weak and strong, would act to defend them, not to make them unemployed.

Tom Paine wrote of the unifying value of a national debt[3], but when foreigners own, as is now the case, well over a third of it, we have to remember that interest rates are set by the lender, and that debts can be called.

Mr. Bush and his people are antisocial in their loathing of, or at very best indifference to, what is "public." That is—or may be—a symptom, a metaphor, of something yet bigger, more malignant. The concept of the totality of us sustaining each of us has no resonance in their minds. In one crucial case, they are blind to or antagonistic of the "social" in Social Security. They would make inroads on what has been one of the great unifying statutes of the republic, on the problematic grounds that individuals could invest their Social Security taxes more profitably for themselves. The pooling of our money for common benefit means nothing to them.

It is these oligarchic class warriors that Mr. Bush's tax policies serve. "It is certainly true that one major by-product of the President's tax-cutting spree to benefit the rich is the impoverishment of federal government, to make it impossible to afford programs to help lower-income Americans. Not far down the road will come crocodile tears and apologies that we're sorry we can't be helpful, but we just can't afford it." Peter Edelman goes on to say, "There are eighty million or so Americans who just can't pay all their bills every month even though they work as hard as they can."[4]

The wealthy know that in the Bush administration they are in control, and they want to stay that way, so they pour unbelievable amounts of money into Mr. Bush's election campaign. "The single factor virtually all [large] donors have in common is that they, their clients, their corporations, their suppliers and their subcontractors are major beneficiaries of the Bush administration's tax-cutting and deregulatory policies. Almost all of the Bush fund-raisers are in the top one percent of the nation's incomes, and many are in the top one-tenth of the top one percent."[5] As the first George Bush might say, this inequality "will not stand."

The second Mr. Bush's determination to rule by embedded theory is on full display in his administration's grappling with traditional civil rights issues. He missed out, as for one reason or another did well nigh all of his lieutenants in their youthful days, on the electrifying experience of participation in the civil rights movement of previous decades and its truly revolutionary impact on American society. None of its passions and idealism touched him and his people.

So he started, as is his usual radical practice, by rejecting what has been: "liberal" policies must yield, his administration insists, to ones better suited to our "values," and this requires new people. Civil rights leaders who have risen through established organizational processes are ignored as he deals through his own chosen advisors. Our old liberal policies are certainly not perfect, and the men and women who have been long committed to the civil rights and antipoverty movement struggles for equal opportunity know better than these Republicans their shortcomings. But only a fringe of advocates trust this administration's solutions.

The administration has chosen to attack affirmative action, has denigrated the case for school integration, has flaunted its program for school vouchers, has opposed hard-won job rules, has opposed the civic rights of residents of the nation's capital city (predominantly African-American and other minorities), has shown little interest in low-priced housing for the homeless, has treated the Commission on Civil Rights insultingly—in all that it does it is the opposite of fair or unifying.

RULE OF LAW. Mr. Bush and his administration define who is and who is not a patriot in terms that come close to excluding all but their kind of Republicans. As they see it, unity is first of all support of the Commander-in-Chief (which is the practical, the operative meaning of the mantra: support our troops); an acceptance of the claim that the primary responsibility for foreign policy rests with the Commander-in-Chief, which is to say acceptance of the militarization of foreign policy; a conviction that our large corporations are rightful and essential members of American society whose interests must always be enriched and nurtured; and that the federal government's principal, indeed almost sole, functions are military and so-called homeland security, and enforcement of supportive laws.

Several hundreds of thousands of Americans took to the streets and other public places in the months before the launching of war in March 2003 to plead and demand that war not happen. Mr. Bush did not give them the courtesy of notice. In his defiance of huge numbers of his fellow citizens, he has attempted to rule with no effort at conciliation (nor has he changed, as evidence pours upon us that those protesters—not he—were right and patriotic in the prewar days).

Republicanism has also become habituated to elevating the presidency, and its present occupant, to a level of unquestioned authority, and Mr. Bush has not been reluctant to make the ascension; *vide*. the mad fantasy of his aircraft carrier landing on May 1 to proclaim victory over Iraq, and his Thanksgiving 2003 flight to Baghdad bearing a show turkey.

This ego-tripping has become standard practice. An interview on French television on May 29 was typical: "I'm not mad—I mean I'm disappointed and the American people are disappointed—I can understand—the French intelligence service has been very good to work with—and for that I'm grateful—the first thing I want to do [in a meeting with Arab leaders] is to make it very clear—that I am intent—I want them to look me in the eye so they can see I am determined—"; etc.[6] So it goes.

The American plan of government both allows and requires a powerful chief executive. A resulting by-product is elevated grandeur, inviting presidents to accept and act upon exalted station. We bestow, in the normal course of things, a readily available supply of trust in his (or someday, her) leadership. So as a people we hurt when we are lied to by presidents, as Mr. Nixon came to do, and as Mr. Johnson did in taking us into war and the consequent deaths of many thousands. Their offices (and their parties') were the price these men paid. Mr. Bush lied to us in order to war against Iraq. Did he personally do that knowingly?

"Contrary to the impression created by the administration," Mr. Warren Christopher said on November 27, 2003,[7] "Iraq was not responsible for the Sept. 11 attacks, and there was no proof that Iraq was in league with al-Qaeda. Similarly, Niger did not sell uranium to Iraq, Iraq was not on the cusp of nuclear capability, and Saddam Hussein did not have at-the-ready stores of weapons of mass destruction. In sum, the United States launched a preemptive war without convincing evidence that Iraq" was an imminent threat to our nation.

This conception of unity as "support of the commander-in-chief" puts little importance on much that historically has been considered part of the American *res publica*. Schools, libraries, conservation of our natural resources, parks, hospitals, social insurance, welfare—in this new Republicanism these are nice things to have perhaps, but not essential and better abandoned by the federal government—in current terminology, "privatized."

In this new dogma, the fifty state governments and local governments have their usefulness, but must accept that the federal role in law enforcement will expand and that the military's prerogatives are supreme. The Department of Homeland Security is another long step along the way of the *national security state* becoming the *nation*, subordinating to itself all the institutions of civil society—even universities and churches, and of course labor unions—on its way.

From the republic's first days until the Civil War its most momentous issue had been the defense of the union from division. Some truly awful compromises were made in order to keep the Southern states from breaking loose: the 3/5ths provision; the continuation of slave importation until 1808; the persecution of runaway slaves. These concessions to the Southern states were in the Constitution itself. Later came the Missouri Compromise; the Kansas-Nebraska Act; the Compromise of 1850. One of the old compromises within the Constitution still bedevils the polity: the Electoral College.

The South historically has been the great divider. As the region and the Republican Party now sit astride each other, the South's capability for dividing the polity into two nations flourishes; not this time a territorial division but a division over what America means.

The Civil War behind us, by the end of the nineteenth century most people had come to think of themselves simply as Americans. The creed of patriotism and its firm tenets were then invented, as surrogate for common nativity and history. Without the long histories of European nations, and responding to the waves of immigrants making homes here, American nationhood was self-consciously fashioned from symbolic meanings, chief among them being the sanctity of the Constitution. The import of that is clear: tampering with its venerated status weakens national unity.

But the Bush administration is no respecter of the Constitution. The shamefully misnamed Patriot Act is a virtual assault on the Constitution. In fairness, it has to be said that earlier Congresses and presidents were culpable too, though not to the same measure, and some of their wrongdoing—such as the Foreign Intelligence Surveillance Court—has been obsessively enlarged by Attorney General Ashcroft and this Republican Congress.

Mr. Bush shows too his low valuation of the Constitution, in particular the separation of powers, by continually forcing division, sending to the Senate judicial nominations of persons who have records of disrespect for established law, and who are calculatedly certain to provoke fierce controversy.

Respect for law, for the rule of law, is absolutely fundamental to the search for a "more perfect union." Flagwaving and bumper stickers bespeak a flabby and fragile patriotism. They are poor and gimmicky substitutes for vital civic institutions. Good public schools, fine libraries, well-kept parks, loving care of the God-given nature that surrounds, are the sort of public possessions and heritage that bind the citizenry.

AVOIDANCE OF IDEOLOGY. The twentieth century was for civilization a long trial by ordeal of wars and political bestiality. It also, however, saw the road to "life, liberty, and the pursuit of happiness" open as never before for multitudes around the globe. The worldwide journey to political freedom—in South Africa, India, eastern Europe, Latin America, elsewhere—is, we can reasonably hope, unstoppable. America has been a vital carrier of the progress through the women's suffrage movement; the civil rights movement; the ensuing drives by Mexican-Americans, Indians, several Asian groups, homosexuals; and, of huge import, a resurgent women's movement for equal privilege. This is the America to be loved, the land meant when one sings "my country 'tis of thee, sweet land of liberty." The glory of America historically has been its openness to new people, and to new ideas. The advance of freedom is probably its own forward engine, though it would be consistent with our country's ideals to do what all of us can do to help it along.

It is a force that makes puny men such as the House majority leader, Tom DeLay of Texas, who chastises Democrats for not recognizing that "our nation is genuinely threatened by a real and dangerous evil, the destruction of which must be *the single unifying purpose of our nation.*" [8]

The White House's single-minded war on "terrorism" needs to be prosecuted with active awareness that although "terrorists" may not be nice or good people they are acting against what they perceive to be harsh infringements of their rights and freedoms. Some rightful portion of our attitude toward them must—must, if we have a concern for the future tomorrows—be a grudging respect, for them as it for like reason must be for the Johnny Rebs and other nativist radicals among us.

Government by consent in the United States was not even a theoretical possibility prior to the civil rights movement. Dating from it there has occurred the real "nation building" time of the republic, and it still goes on. Millions of persons have entered into our social contract. A basic part of that contract was that terrorism was to end in the United States.

Terrorism had been for three centuries the ultimate and oft-used method in the Southern states for holding down their black members. It had also been by terror that Indians, Mexican-Americans, Filipinos, and at one time or another other minorities were brutally oppressed. Terrorism, however defined, is nothing new. Getting rid of Mr. Saddam Hussein was a worthwhile achievement, unless the price that is being and will be paid is too heavy. But in itself, his removal does not control the plague of brutal violence that has been and is humanity's curse.

Mr. Bush and his administration proudly call themselves conservative. They need to listen to Edmund Burke, by general agreement the greatest conservative voice of English-speaking societies.

"Society," he wrote, "is indeed a contract. Subordinate contracts for objects of mere occasional interest may be dissolved at pleasure, but the state ought not to be considered as nothing better than a partnership agreement in a trade of pepper and coffee [oil and natural gas], calico or tobacco [textiles or computer programs], or some other such low concern, to be taken up for a little temporary interest, and to be dissolved by the fancy of the parties. It is to be looked on with other reverence; because it is not a partnership in things subservient only to the gross animal existence of a temporary and perishable nature. It is a partnership in all science; a partnership in all art; a partnership in every virtue, and in all perfection. As the ends of such a partnership cannot be obtained in many generations, it becomes a partnership not only between those who are living, but between those who are living, those who are dead, and those who are to be born."[9]

We might appropriately add that the onrushing twenty-first century's global society will either be a similar "partnership"—in all that is civilizing—or humanity may be doomed. The presidents we need will be ones understanding of that, leaders whose bent is toward making whole and away from seeing the world's peoples as separated, us and them, good and bad.

Mr. Bush and his friends speak often of their conviction in favor of "faith-based" programs. They do not extend their liking of such to "faith-based" opposition to the government's war-making programs. Here too Mr. Bush's predilection for division is present. Among Christian churches, as well as among worshippers of other faiths, there is diversity of opinion, but it is safe to say that virtually none of the large, so-called mainline religious organizations except the Southern Baptists approve of the Iraqi war; nor, in fact, approved of the earlier war against Iraq led by the first Bush. On questions of war and peace, few opinions weigh less in current political scales than those of "faith-based" institutions.

Mr. Bush describes his policies as "compassionate conservatism." That was and is a shoddy slogan to proclaim and boast of. Whatever it may mean, it is an unworthy political ideal. Compassion is a good and necessary practice for strong (or rich) individuals toward weak (or poor) ones: we usually call that charity. It is a good practice for victor nations—militarily or economically—toward loser nations. But it is a completely wrong and demeaning attitude, policy, or practice of a government toward fellow citizens, fellow partners in their social contract.

For most of the world's people—*i.e.*, the poor—"freedom" may be a lesser word and value than "equality." It is the demand to be equal, to be accorded equal respect and dignity and opportunity, that is driving struggles in Palestine and other Arab lands, in Latin America, in Africa, in all the other battlegrounds of the world. It was a people's determination to be equal that defeated the United States in Vietnam. That same kind of determination to be equally valued will defeat and, in near time, drive us from Iraq. We have no "manifest destiny" to rendezvous within that faraway place. And we will lose, as we presume to claim one.

The modern Republican ideology requires belief in American supremacy—of our power, privilege, morality, of our right, independent of the claims or criticisms of other governments and peoples. In civil rights days, the white South tended to brush off world opinion, and especially that of those living beyond the north Atlantic areas. The white Southern-led current Republican Party espouses similar unilateralism. It is the old South's ideology of white supremacy, now writ large and become Republican USA supremacy. ∎

Beyond Capitalism

JANISSE RAY

"But it left something with him; as long as the hummingbird had not abandoned the land, somewhere there were still flowers, and they could all go on." —Leslie Marmon Silko, *Ceremony*

EVERY OCTOBER, mostly without our knowing it, ruby-throated hummingbirds migrate across the southlands, heading to the Florida coast and across the Gulf to overwinter—a wave of living jewels shimmering south, pausing at the last trumpet flowers and honeysuckle.

This year the Audubon Society's new nature center near Holly Springs, Mississippi, had its first hummingbird migration festival. Biologist Bob Sargent came with live traps and tiny pliers so that hundreds of people could watch volunteer bird-banders squeeze little silver bands on the legs of limp hummingbirds. My friend Ann stood so long at the table, mesmerized, that finally, after the calibrating and inspecting and recording was done, she got to release one of the birds. She held it in her flat palm like a child might, feeling its dewdrop of a heart race with life. Without notice it rose, shook out its miniature blue-green cloak of wings, and vanished.

Later we sat at a bird window and watched a hymn of hummingbirds, each a note rising and falling, clamoring over the feeders and the salvia: males with their red throats, females of a green so iridescent and luminous I wanted to weep.

Every year, I thought, watching them, despite what we do to

the landscape, despite what we destroy and steal, despite the diminishment of what they depend upon, the hummingbirds keep coming. In spring they fly north, where they build delicate teacup homes out of moss and lichens, and there, following elaborate mating rituals, they lay eggs hardly bigger than jelly beans. They raise impossibly tiny offspring. Late fall they fly south, over strip developments and eight-lane highways, over herbicide-laden cotton fields and kudzu-wrapped gullies, over sprawl, over clearcut forests, over the heads of human beings—who on festival day are buying birdhouses, hiking the trail to the slave graves, or bumping along on hay rides through the preserve.

Above our heads the hummingbirds pass unnoticed.

FOR MOST OF MY short life I have been alarmed—that is the word—by the hemorrhaging of wild things from this planet. I have spent a lot of time conversing, reading and thinking: what is the root of this loss and how might we stem it? Lack of education, some said, especially in science and the environment: teach the children. We don't have time to wait for the children, others said. We need change now: teach the adults. Was the problem a Christian attitude of dominion over the earth? Was the problem rural attitudes—rednecks killing snakes, Crackers cutting forests, hillbillies heedlessly mining their coal? Was overpopulation our main worry?

I kept thinking that if we could find the one thing that most contributed to the destruction, and put our minds and bodies to

---

Political activist JANISSE RAY is author of *Ecology of a Cracker Childhood* and *Wild Card Quilt: Taking a Chance on Home*. A native of the pine flatwoods of south Georgia, Ray was the Grisham writer-in-residence at the University of Mississippi during 2003–04.

work to remedy that, we would do the most good, given ignorance and timidity and fear, and the brevity of a human life span. Most people want to do the most good in the shortest amount of time.

I used to think that if we saved enough wild places, and we changed enough public policy, that we could stop environmental degradation: extinctions of species, fragmentation of habitat, pollution, toxification of water and air, and so forth. We could keep natural processes intact. As an activist and as an environmentalist, I worked hard, and with some success, for these things.

On my fortieth birthday, some months after September 11, 2001, my thinking changed. My husband and I traveled to Mexico to see the overwintering place of monarch butterflies. Two weeks before, unbeknownst to us as we planned our trip, a killing frost one January night had swept through the Sierra Madre range. In cold weather monarch butterflies mass together in thick gray combs on tree limbs. As temperatures plummeted, they loosened from their clusters and dropped like fall leaves to the forest floor, dead. Millions fell. The next morning the ground was covered with a carpet of butterfly bodies, in places a foot thick, a cemetery of monarchs.

This phenomenon had happened because trees in the area continued to be cut, until they were no longer able to provide the protection that the butterflies needed. Maybe global climate change had something to do with the weather. One freeze, and an entire population of already threatened butterfly was in jeopardy.

Back in the little tile-floored, stucco hotel in El Rosario, my husband and I read Wendell Berry's book, "In the Presence of Fear," aloud to each other. We had brought it along on our travels because it was small, and lightweight. Nothing about the contents of Berry's book fit those adjectives. The book, three essays written in the aftermath of the 9/11 attacks, was a long hard look at our country's reputation globally, our economic system of plunder at home and abroad, and the alternatives we face.

My eyes were opened.

WE IN THE UNITED STATES have been true believers in our industrial capitalistic economic system, Berry writes. Even as climate changes globally and polar ice caps melt and seas inch higher along coastlines worldwide, we cling to the belief that capitalism will bring prosperity to all the world, starting with ourselves. Lost in this idea of prosperity, wooed by industrialism's trinkets and gadgets, we fail to see that industrial capitalism, which we have now managed to spread globally, cannot forever go on producing more and more. Industrial capitalism is based on a model of an uphill line, so that we expect more and more: more prosperity, more money from the pocketful we invest in stocks, more profit. Thus our fixation on "growth." This ever-increasing "return" to us always comes at the expense of local ecosystems, local communities, local economies, and local cultures. Always.

As Berry writes, global capitalist industrialization is an inherently violent system, since it destroys everything on which it depends. It is going to fail because it is a system that requires more and more of itself to solve its own problems. The earth cannot forever or even for long sustain this depletion of resources.

Nor does our economic system mean ever-increasing prosperity for all, but for the few. The prosperity, Berry writes, is "limited to a tiny percentage of the world's people, and to an ever smaller number of people even in the United States; that it was founded on the oppressive labor of poor people all over the world; and that its ecological costs increasingly threaten all life, including the lives of the supposedly prosperous."

We residents of the "First-World" nations are making great sacrifices to this idea of ever-increasing prosperity for ourselves-we give to it our health, the reality of childhood, our elders, our natural and cultural heritage, our wholeness, and sometimes even our sanity. As we march deeper into a global capitalist economy, we give up our farmlands, our farmers, our rural communities, our forests and grasslands, our ecosystems and watersheds, and the lives of poor workers around the globe. We accept global warming, universal pollution, an increase in illnesses, and species extinctions as the justified costs of doing business.

We unwittingly give global corporations proxy to provide whatever we desire as cheaply as possible. In most cases, we have no idea what goes into the production of items we buy, the true cost to us or to others or to the earth in terms of health and wholeness and damage, nor who or what suffered in the production. This is especially true of our food, the most fundamental of necessities: most of it arrives heavily fertilized and pesticide-laden, gassed or waxed, irradiated, treated with hormones or steroids, highly processed, or genetically modified; and from a very long distance, requiring a tremendous use of fossil fuels. Corporate production of food comes at great expense to our land, our rural communities, and to our own bodies.

In the face of the loss that surrounds and engulfs us, we desperately cling to our moral notion of the sanctity of life, with a dedication that is often little more than lip-service, and to the remnants of those things that have made sense to us.

Back home from Mexico, we kept reading: Arundhati Roy, Vandana Shiva, Howard Zinn, Alice Walker, Greg Palast, E. F. Schumacher, Noam Chomsky, Gore Vidal, Barbara Kingsolver, until I knew the thing to be true.

THE ROOT CAUSE of our environmental undoing is our economic system of industrial capitalism.

Discussion of capitalism often makes people nervous, because it seems completely unpatriotic, and most of us love our country.

I am quick to point out that global industrial capitalism is our *economic* system in the United States, not our *political* system, which is democracy and which I would defend, in its true form, loudly and fiercely, until death.

And the information is not easy to hear. To acknowledge that our culpability was greater than we knew, to be implicated in the destruction of that which we hold most dear, to accuse ourselves: these are hard feelings to face.

Everywhere I go now to lecture, I talk about capitalism. After I spoke to the 2003 North Carolina Native Plant Society conference, when the question-and-answer session began, a man came up on stage. He walked with a cane. He limped up beside me to the microphone and stood there. No one had ever done this, and I did not know if I should be frightened. "Hello," I said to him, through the microphone.

"I want to give you something," he said. "I want to thank you for speaking for me." The man had begun to weep. "I don't have much, but I'd like to give you my hat, if you'd accept it. It's the only one I have and it means a lot to me, but I'd like you to have it."

He held out a ball cap, dyed black. On its front was embroidered the Native American symbols of the four elements.

"Thank you very much," I said, accepting his gift, although I seldom wear ball caps. "I'll treasure it."

He tapped slowly back off the stage and up the immense stairs of the auditorium to his seat. The first real question came from a man midway the audience. He demanded to know if I realized that I was one of the prosperous—I had benefited from human advances, such as the discovery of penicillin, I had driven to the conference by automobile, I ate good food.

Before I could think of the truthful answer, the man who had delivered his gift-hat to me retorted, then another older gentleman stood up and began yelling at the man with the cane, until I thought a fight would break out. I let the yelling continue a few minutes, first because I didn't know what to do, and secondly, because I think we need to be able to engage in dialogue about an issue so shocking to hear about and so vital to our survival. When the debate on the floor began to dissolve into insults, I simply began to read a passage from my book: *What thrills me most about longleaf forests is how the pine trees sing.*

When I ended, the audience rose for a standing ovation. Lights are coming on in people's eyes everywhere.

WHEN WE KNOW A PROBLEM, the nature of the human mind forces us to seek solution. I have learned four possible approaches to a doomed economic system that will not ensure our long-term survival:

> One, we can keep on the path we're on. Wendell Berry again: "We can continue to promote a global economic system of unlimited "free trade" among corporations, . . . now recognizing that such a system will have to be protected by a hugely expensive police force that will be worldwide . . . and that such a police force will be effective precisely to the extent that it oversways the freedom and privacy of the citizens of every nation." We will be the subject of more terrorist attacks.
>
> Two, basically, as is, we have created a system of liars and thieves, who get away with murder. We can imbue capitalism with the ethics it has forgotten, which was what even Thomas Jefferson called for, in setting up the government of the country. So that we create a system where we have learned to say "enough." Where nobody is oppressed or exploited in the name of profit or anything else. Where scandals like Enron will not happen. Where, if they do, justice will be served.
>
> Three, maybe we could dismantle industrialism altogether

and come up with a new system. Communism didn't produce enough. Capitalism produces too much, resulting in an astonishingly wasteful society, too many cheap products winding up in local landfills. Could a task force of the smartest people living right now come up with a true world order? Maybe *sustainabilism?*

Let me stress that I did not see the problem first myself, nor have I seen a solution. I was shown the problem. I am a person awakened, a Southern woman writer who loves her homeland, awakened to a dire situation. I am no longer looking at regional causes for the loss of our Southern landscapes. I am looking globally and I am looking within.

Four, this seems the best solution. This is the one my husband and I have chosen, and continue to choose daily. *We can promote local economics, meaning that every place is charged with a local self-sufficiency in the production of necessary goods and services.* Economies would be decentralized, not global. Stock. Stockholders would not pillage worldwide. International trade would still be feasible, but it would mostly involve the exchange of surpluses after local needs had been met. Countries would pass and support local measures to promote sustainability; other nations would honor those measures. Dangerous and misleading agreements like the North American Free Trade Agreement and the Free Trade Agreement of the Americas would be dismantled.

A local self-sufficiency. Or, as I like to say, a local co-sufficiency. A local economics.

ONE YEAR AGO, after twenty-six years as a letter carrier with the postal service, without retirement benefits (not for thirteen years, anyway) and without fanfare, my husband, Raven, quit his job.

On his last day of work, the automatons of postal officials would not allow me even to send a chocolate cake to honor the twenty-six years of his life he had given to the mail service.

Raven and I had only been married six months when he quit his boring, thankless, federal government job. We moved back to my family farm in southern Georgia, our permanent address, where I had been living when I met Raven and which had been the subject of my second book, *Wild Card Quilt: Taking a Chance on Home*. Our goals:

1. to live as simply as we could manage;
2. to live within our means (stay out of debt);
3. to produce as much for ourselves as possible;
4. to avoid buying what we didn't absolutely need;
5. beyond that, to buy as locally as possible;
6. to try never to shop in chain stores, especially not Wal-Mart, which is now our nation's largest company based on revenues and the nineteenth largest economy in the world; and
7. to cut down on fossil fuel use, hopefully to reduce it by 30 percent over the following couple of years.

Life, oh this beautiful life, it opened to us in a way we had never thought possible.

THE CHICKEN BUSINESS WAS NEW TO ME. When we purchased a dozen chicks in early spring, I had to learn from scratch how to take care of them, the kind of feed to buy, and how to keep them safe from bobcats. Slowly they grew. Finally the beautiful chanticleer began to crow, tentatively at first then announcing each sunrise in earnest. At first terrified of me, his beautiful collection of hens began to associate my clucking with a handful of lettuce stems or leftover rice.

One day I went to throw the chickens a bowl of cantaloupe pulp, full of seeds, and found the first egg, small, brown and dirty, laying right in the middle of the pen. The first egg! I looked around and found another beside the feed bucket, which overflowed with cracked corn.

My husband admired the eggs and went out to have a look himself. A few minutes later I heard the door open. "You missed an egg," he said.

"Oh yeah?" I asked carelessly, looking up. He was holding a long oak snake tangled in his hands. A third egg, apparently uncracked, lay lodged in the snake's midsection.

"Well," I said, "I guess we lost that one." Raven deposited the snake in a bucket to relocate it down the dirt road to another habitat.

We were proud of our first golden eggs. They meant more to us than eggs.

We acquired wild hogs, planted fruit trees, and tripled the size of the garden both of us had always kept. A farmer gave us bales of spoiled hay for mulch, an attorney supplied manure from his horse barn. For a long time, so we could track our patterns of spending, we kept a daily log of purchases, anything over one dollar. Even the simple act of writing down expenses in the evening would make us think twice before making a purchase. We insulated the old farmhouse, and got a free load of lumber from the local lumber supply, which was trying to clean out a building, lumber that we hoped to use for repairs on outbuildings and the farmhouse, and for building a workshop.

In late August we took one of those Americana portraits of ourselves. We are standing in rubber boots, ramrod straight, holding familiar pitchfork and shovel upright, in front of one day's bounty—buckets of rattlesnake beans, a few melons, candy roaster squashes, blemished tomatoes, bell peppers, two or three watermelons, eggplant, a handful of basil and rosemary for pesto.

Each day we harvest what seems like a truckload of food. In the picture Raven couldn't keep the smile off his face but I am looking very severe.

Hunting season finds us in a tree stand on our friend Milton's farm before dawn, watching the shadowy trees for a lone deer to come walking toward us. My husband and I love deer, and watch them all year. Taking one for meat is not a sport for us. Raven is a crack shot, able to kill without wounding, and we spend a day then thanking the earth for the gift of a deer, butchering the beautiful animal, and processing every part of the animal possible, sometimes even the hide.

Most of our meals are home-cooked. Every time we sit down to a meal there is a moment of reckoning when we look at our steaming, colorful plates, and take note of what percentage of the meal we produced. For supper one winter night my husband broils a sea bass he caught one weekend out of the Gulf of Mexico, with tarragon from the garden and butter from the store. I steam pole beans we put in the freezer back before the vines succumbed to July's heat. Nothing in the salad we grew. We give ourselves a 50.

Sometimes, entire meals come from our own hands and from the miracle of life. That's a good feeling, not only because we're doing our little part to oppose global capitalism, but we know our food has been grown without pesticides and herbicides and mostly without the use of fossil fuels. And it tastes great.

Sometimes, all of a meal is store-bought.

We are not trying to be self-sufficient, but something closer to co-sufficient. We want to be part of a community of people providing for ourselves and each other.

It's a lot of work. But it is good work, holy work, happy work, probably our life's work. Doing it, we are ecstatic.

For Christmas last year, our wonderful teenage son gave me a small box of feathers so small and airy that I have to hold my breath when I look at them. A ruby-throated hummingbird had hit his bedroom window, and died, and, before burying it, he had collected a box of its feathers. The present was wrapped and waiting for me on Christmas morning, a gift more dear than anything money could buy. If hummingbirds have not abandoned the land, somewhere there are flowers.

ALL OVER THE COUNTRY, people are working on systems of local economies: Alternative dollars. Barter fairs. Biodiesel. Solar power. Community-supported agriculture. Slow-food gatherings. Potlucks. Local business enterprise. Farmers' markets.

Bless them.

Then join them.

My husband and I are not heroes in this mission of living simply. We are not angels. We love to travel. We love a new pair of good shoes.

We have, however, made a conscious decision to shop less and consume less and run around less. We think twice about consumption: Do we really need this? Can we do without it? Will what we already own suffice? Is it better to keep our eleven-year-old pickup or to save toward one of the new hybrid cars? Where was the product made? What people or wildlife or communities suffered that we could own this? What will benefit from this purchase? Is the item biodegradable? Recyclable?

In our efforts, we have to oppose a culture addicted to newness. North Americans want everything they own, from automobiles to zany shoes, to appear brand-new; so that they (who is we) have developed a kind of despise for the dented, the rusty, the worn-down, the outdated. I am reminded of William Faulkner, and of the photos taken of him in the most ragged coat and pants imaginable. For the most part, most of us miss the beauty in repair; we are forgetting how to repair—how to use needle and thread, glue, nails and hammer, plain old wire.

The documentary about living simply, *Affluenza*, claims that if everyone in the entire world were afforded the lifestyles we Americans now enjoy, we would need three or four planets to sustain us.

To oppose a system that we have considered our birthright and our patria is going to take tremendous courage. I think of the elderly woman I once saw driving an old Mercury down an interstate highway. A sign in her back window read, 397,000 miles and still going. She meant the car. I feel that way about mine. We have 215,000 miles on the little Toyota pickup and it's still running strong. Until it quits, I do not intend to part with it. Maybe when it does we will be able to afford a hybrid, or maybe we will have created a lifestyle that does not require a vehicle at all.

Television plays a major role in keeping us trapped in our consumptive culture. It keeps us in a trance of materialism, promotes violence, robs time better spent with our families and our communities, and fails to give us accurate reporting on events and significances in the world. Which is why our family has chosen not to watch television.

When George W. Bush became president (albeit not by popular vote), his chosen administration amped up actions that endangered the future of life on earth, and promoted the principles of overconsumption, global capitalism and media lies. We could see the ills of our times up close then, with our own eyes. Often, hearing the news, we could not believe our ears. Bush's Cabinet was stocked with industrialists, not scientists. Not thinkers. We worried about the rolling back of environmental regulations, the passing of late-night bills, the power granted the "free trade" tribunals, the ignoring of United Nations agreements, the robbery of our freedoms. We were ashamed and angry that President Bush wouldn't sign the Kyoto Treaty. We couldn't believe that he would lead our country into an invasion of Iraq for the acquisition of oil, in order to insure the continuation of our consumerist culture.

I got invited to do a writing stint in Oxford, Mississippi, so we closed down the farm—sold the pigs, lent the chickens to friends—and left for nine months. Not for good. In Oxford we continued our efforts to bolster the local economy—we shopped at locally owned businesses, we bought produce at the farmer's market and from local organic farmers, we rode bicycles more than we drove the truck. One week I picked up Helen and Scott Nearing's book, *Living the Good Life*. The Nearings in the 1930s left New York City for what they called Third-World America, meaning rural Vermont. They bought a farm and began to set up a life there that was beyond what they called the "profit economy." They saw very clearly what the Depression had done; people who were dependent on wages suddenly lost their jobs, and were divorced then from the sources of their survival. The Nearings prove that a local economy is possible. Their book is a kind of Bible for us. It is comfort when we miss the farm.

ON THE WAY HOME to Oxford from the hummingbird migration festival, both of us on the motorcycle, and hungry, we stopped at a restaurant called Annie's in Holly Springs. It was a large, peach-brick place, recently built. I should tell you first about Holly Springs. Its downtown functions not as a tourist lure (as Oxford's square has become) but as a real center: drugstore, cafes, hardware store, grocery. On the Holly Springs square, you still see people who belong to both of the major races down here. On the square in Oxford, you see mostly white people, buying silk scarves and cappuccino, having drinks on the balcony of City Grocery.

Inside Annie's, a young woman showed us to a booth and invited us to partake of the buffet lunch. We did, heaping thick white plates high with fried catfish, turnip greens, sweet potato souffle, crackling cornbread. Our waiter brought us water and coffee.

I would not normally mention the color of her skin. It was the lovely smoothness of dark chocolate. She was wearing a T-shirt with a picture of a man on it, a memorial, she said, to her uncle, a fun-loving, favorite uncle who was killed six months before on a motorcycle. She looked at us with odd concern as she told the story; she had seen us come in with helmets under our arms.

"We've never heard of this restaurant," we said to her. "Is it a chain?"

"No," she said.

"So it's locally owned?" I asked.

"It's owned by a beautiful woman named Annie," she replied, smiling impishly. "Sitting right over there." She indicated a table toward the kitchen door where a couple of workers were rolling silverware inside napkins.

"Which one?"

"The one in white."

Annie was indeed a beautiful woman in her forties who looked like a queen, her hair impeccably coiffed, her ivory suit flattering and lovely against caramel-colored skin.

"Please tell her we're proud to be eating with her."

While we ate I watched Annie speak to people as they entered. I watched her move from table to table, chatting with diners. Before long, she came to us.

"How are y'all doing?"

We told her how we try to support only locally owned businesses, how that gets harder all the time to do, how wonderful her food tasted, how beautiful her restaurant looked. She stood close to our table, smiling, cheerful.

"I was a hairdresser," she said. "I wanted a restaurant but I didn't have the means to build one. I borrowed money to construct this building. I thought, 'I'm going on faith.' And so I built it. It was a miracle. God has blessed me, for me to be able to create all this."

Annie was poised and elegant. "You know what I mean?" she said to me, and touched my shoulder.

"I do. How many people do you employ?"

"About a dozen," she said.

"Well, you run a lovely business," I said. "We're glad to know you're here."

"I try to touch everyone who comes in," Annie said. "I will minister to them and bless them, if they need that, but I mean literally, I try to touch them. Give them a hug or put my hand on their arm. They keep coming back."

Annie excused herself then. Her mother had entered, with her sister and a couple of younger family members, maybe nieces, not to eat but to drop by and say hello. Our waiter came back with pecan pie.

NOT LONG AGO I NEEDED a last skein of embroidery thread for a set of flannel pillowcases I was making for two friends who were marrying. We were traveling to the ceremony, passing through a small town in the hills of northern Georgia. At a gas station we asked a fellow where we might find such an item as a small skein of gold embroidery thread. "The only place around here is Wal-Mart," he said. We kept driving, and in the next town stopped at two or three local stores. None of them stocked embroidery thread. That afternoon I finally gave fifty cents to Mall-Wart. I hope it was my last.

I was reminded of the cloth store in Oxford where I had purchased the fabric for the pillowcases. It was a Saturday, near quitting time, and the woman who owned the store was there, along with her daughter, who helped her wait on customers, as were two of her grown sons, who had come to see their mother home.

"Are you new to Oxford?" she asked as she cut the green cotton.

"We're here for nine months," I said.

"You must be the writer-in-residence."

"I am."

"I'm proud to meet you," she said. "My name's Eileen. I did the draperies in the house you're living in. And the linens. If you need anything sewed, I'd be glad to help you."

"I'll be back."

"And be careful on your bicycle on the way home."

Eileen's is the kind of business I want to frequent, her cordiality is the response I want to get to my presence in a place of business, her family is the kind I want to support with my dollars.

I HAVE DEDICATED my life to wildness. My path in the world, my calling, is to be a voice for the beleaguered Southern landscape. I write out of love for my place, and out of love for all places beloved to humans. Because of this great love, I am an activist: my goal is to help remake this ship we call Earth so that on it we may practice what it means to be fully human. So that we may belong to a world in which it is possible to know our full humanity. Not everybody has to suddenly buy forty acres in the country and install solar panels. But we all have to be aware that as consumers, as seekers of prosperity, we are not only guilty of the destruction of our world, we are charged with the task of remaking it. We must educate ourselves about the consequences of our daily lives. Our dollars are votes. The world needs thinkers, not consumers.

In hundreds of ways every day, we have the option to make decisions that either add to global warming, biological extinction and pollution, or prolong and strengthen life on earth, including our own. These decisions can be as small as turning out a light, or as big as deciding not to have another child, or voting for a candidate who believes in life, or not building a new house on an undeveloped piece of land. Every day we have the chance to act courageously and ethically. We are very powerful then. This is the most important piece of knowledge we can be given. This work—the chance to act courageously and ethically—is the most vital work of our time.

Tell people about what you're doing. There is no need to be apologetic about decisions that favor the earth. Your stories will add to the body of knowledge of how we can lead whole, sustainable, love-filled lives amid fragmentation and loss.

The hummingbirds are in our hands. ∎

Civil Liberties in a Time of Crises: The Dark Side

Daniel H. Pollitt

Thomas Jefferson was referring to slavery when he wrote, "I tremble for my country when I reflect that God is Just."[1] Were he alive today he might well repeat the same words about how the Bush administration has run amok over the Constitution the founders nurtured, and how few seem to care. Robert Byrd of West Virginia said on the Senate floor:

> "To contemplate war is to think about the most horrible of human experiences.... Yet this chamber is, for the most part silent—ominously, dreadfully silent. There is no debate, no discussion. There is nothing.[2]

Jefferson might well worry that so few respond to James Madison's admonition to take alarm at the first incursion on our liberties. However illegal, unconstitutional, or shameful these incursions may be, they hold widespread support.[3]

If challenged to count the ways the Constitution is battered Jefferson could chose from a wide variety.

THE FOURTH AMENDMENT. Our proud boast for more than two hundred years was that "every man's house is his castle." This concept is enshrined in our Fourth Amendment.[4] Listen to the eloquent words of Lord Pitt on the floor of Parliament:

> The poorest man may, in his cottage, bid defiance to all the force of the Crown. It may be frail; its roof may shake; the wind may blow through it; the storm may enter; the rain may enter; but the King of England may not enter; all his force dares not cross the threshold of the ruined tenement.

Pitt spoke in defense of a court decision holding that a homeowner could sue a law officer for searching his dwelling without a warrant. In that decision[5] Lord Camden wrote that were it otherwise:

> the secret cabinets and bureaus of every subject in the kingdom will be thrown open to the search and inspection of a messenger, whenever the secretary of state shall think fit to charge, or even to suspect, a person to be the author, printer, or publisher of a seditious libel.

Despite our heritage, the Bush Administration seems determined to throw open the "cabinets and bureaus of every subject" to the search and seizure of the police.

"SNEAK AND PEEK" (SOME CALL IT BURGLARY). The Ashcroft 342-page Patriot Act, introduced almost immediately after the September 11 bombing, raced through Congress almost unread,

---

DANIEL H. POLLITT is Kenan Professor of Constitutional Law Emeritus, University of North Carolina, Chapel Hill, North Carolina. When on the faculty he frequently left the classroom to serve as defense attorney in capital cases and to represent clients among the poor, disabled, and disenfranchised on issues of free speech and civil liberties.

much less debated.⁶ One of its provisions authorized "sneak and peek" searches of people's homes and further authorized the government to sit on information that a search had occurred. The more the Patriot Act is examined, the greater the protest and call for change. "Sneak and peek" was too much. The House of Representatives voted 309 to 118 in an appropriation bill for a Republican-sponsored measure to block the use of federal money for such searches.⁷

At this writing, it awaited action in the Senate, meanwhile leaving the police free to enter your home, search without end, and fade away in the night leaving no trace.

FISA (THE FOREIGN INTELLIGENCE SURVEILLANCE ACT). During the Nixon Administration, the government indicted three defendants for conspiring to dynamite the Central Intelligence Agency Office in Ann Arbor, Michigan. Prior to trial the defendants filed a motion that the court require the government to disclose any evidence obtained by illegal secret wiretaps, and, if any, to determine whether the entire proceeding was tainted. The government admitted that it had not complied with the Fourth Amendment, but argued that Attorney General John Mitchell had authorized the wiretap and his authorization (on behalf of the president) was sufficient in a case of a domestic internal national security problem.

The Supreme Court rejected this contention because, "The historical judgment, which the Fourth Amendment accepts, is that unreviewed executive discretion may yield too readily to pressure to obtain incriminating evidence and overlook potential invasions of privacy and protected speech."⁸

The Court emphasized two things: first, that it did not "address the issues which may be involved with respect to activities of foreign powers or their agents," and second, the application for a warrant, "could, in sensitive cases, be made to any member of a specially designated court."[9]

These holdings were part of the discussion which culminated in the 1978 Foreign Intelligence Surveillance Act, which created a special court, the FISA Court, with authority to authorize wiretaps when the sole purpose was to obtain foreign intelligence information. Since the evidence obtained could not be used in a criminal case, the Act did not require the Department of Justice to show "probable cause" that a crime was in progress. The Department need only show that the wiretap was "relevant" to an investigation of foreign powers or their agents. The FISA court began in 1979 and operated in secret for the next twenty years. In these secret years the FISA court approved ten thousand applications for warrants, *and never turned down a single request.* The government was not always honest in its requests. The FISA court criticized federal agents for misleading the court on seventy-five occasions during the Clinton Administration (as of September 2000) and an unspecified additional number between September 2000 and March 2001. One misleading request was signed by FBI Director Louis J. Freeh.[10]

The FISA court came to public knowledge when the government applied for a surveillance order against a "United States person" allegedly conspiring in "international terrorism." The FISA court authorized the surveillance but imposed the normal limitation between intelligence gathering and criminal prosecution. Anything learned in the intelligence investigation could not be used in a criminal proceeding.

The government argued that the Patriot Act had eliminated this limitation when it required only that the bugging of a foreign agent be a "significant purpose" for the search warrant rather than "the purpose."

The FISA Court of Review agreed with the government that

the Patriot Act "muddied the landscape" with the change from "the *purpose*" language to a "*significant purpose*" and that this amendment "relaxed a requirement that the government show that its primary purpose was other than criminal prosecution.[11]

With this decision the government can use the relaxed standards for obtaining a search warrant and utilize the fruits of the search in criminal proceedings. The FISA law is now used with increasing frequency against criminals with little or no connection to terrorism: drug traffickers, blackmailers, child pornographers.[12]

In a report on May 2, 2003, Attorney General John Ashcroft said the Justice Department had used FISA secret search warrants a record 1,228 times.[13]

The FISA Court of Review "meets behind a cipher-locked door in a windowless bug-proof, vault-like room guarded twenty-four hours a day on the top floor of the Justice Department.[14] Three United States Court of Appeals judges who sit on the special court are handpicked by Chief Justice Rehnquist. The court meets in secret, and allows only the government to appear before it.[15]

This description harkens back through the centuries to a court "of which there is not the like in any other country." It was composed of high clergy and the chief judges and "met in a chamber the roof there of was decked with images of stars" and became known as the Court of Star Chamber.[16] During the reign of Elizabeth the Court sought out heretical sects and publications for punishment. Typically, John Lilburn, an outspoken Quaker, was called to the court. He refused to swear he would answer all questions about himself or his associates (the oath *ex officio*). No "free born Englishman" he claimed, is "bound by the law to accuse himself." For this obstinacy he was "whipt through the streets from the Fleet to the Pilory." There, he "spoke against Bishops," and the star chamber ordered that he be "gagged, laid alone with irons on his hand and feet." He remained in prison until the Long Parliament abolished the Court in 1641—to no one's dismay.[17]

Courts that issue search warrants behind closed doors without requiring "probable cause" deserve no better fate then the star chamber of yore.

FREEDOM TO READ. Justice Marshall wrote for the Supreme Court that "The right to receive information and ideas, regardless of their social worth, is fundamental to our free society"; and "if the First Amendment means anything, it means that a state has no business telling a man what book he may read."[18]

Section 215 of the Patriot Act requires bookstores and librarians to turn over patron records to the FBI upon request if the FBI secures an order from the secret FISA court.[19]

However, we citizens cannot even know the extent of such searches because of a gag order in the law; section 215 makes it a criminal offense for librarians or book sellers to tell when and why and against whom a search was committed. The University of Illinois surveyed 1,500 libraries. We know that 219 libraries had cooperated with law enforcement requests under Section 215, and 225 had not.[20]

In Broward County, Florida, library director Sam Morrison said the FBI had contacted his office, but he declined to elaborate. The FBI instructed him not to reveal any information about the request.[21]

In May 2003 the Department of Justice reported to Congress that it had contacted fifty libraries nationwide. Librarians, however, believe such contacts have been much more frequent.[22]

On September 18, 2003, Attorney General John Ashcroft announced that the FBI had not yet checked any library records. Accusing the American Library Association of fueling "baseless hysteria," Ashcroft said the number of FBI contact with libraries was zero.[23]

Who to believe?

All this takes us back to the pre-Civil War dark years when Southern states made it criminal to possess anti-slavery tracts. Typically, North Carolina laws made it a crime to circulate "any pamphlet or paper . . . the evident tendency whereof it is to cause slaves to become discontented with the bondage in which they are held." For the first offense, violators would be whipped, put in pillory, and imprisoned for not less than a year. For the second offense, the punishment was death.

Reverend Daniel Worth, a Methodist minister, was indicted under this law when he circulated a book by Hinton Helper called *The Impending Crises*. Among other things, the book recommended the end of slavery and a tax on slave owners to provide transit for the freed slaves back to Africa.

It took a Guilford County jury fifteen minutes to convict. Worth appealed, his bond was repealed, and he slipped out of North Carolina to New York. The authorities apparently wanted to avoid the spectacle of an elderly minister placed in the pillory and whipped. The North Carolina legislature amended the law to make death the punishment for the first offense.

In New York, the Reverend Worth was reunited with Benjamin Hedrick, a chemistry professor fired by the University of North Carolina when he openly supported abolitionist John Freemont for president. Threats of mob violence had forced him to flee the state.[24]

A hundred years or more later the South again panicked when the Supreme Court ordered an end to segregated schools. NAACP lawyers were forbidden to tell church groups their rights under *Brown v. Board of Education*. Schools were closed in the face of integration. Public employees were fired for membership or contributions to the NAACP. White preachers lost their pulpits for urging compliance. And there was mob action, extra-legal action. When Autherine Lucy enrolled at the University of Alabama, a thousand white students took to the streets, and the trustees excluded her for her personal safety. Clennon King applied for admission at Ole Miss and was arrested and committed to the state mental hospital on the ground that any Negro who would seek admission to the University of Mississippi was demonstrably insane. The first African American to apply at the University of Georgia was promptly drafted into the Army.[25]

We are happy to put these matters out of mind.

OFFICE OF STRATEGIC INFLUENCE (FALSEHOOD FROM ON HIGH). During World War II the Allies engaged in a campaign of deception to make the Germans believe Allied forces were making a D-Day landing at Calais, France, instead of Normandy. Vice President Cheney and Secretary of Defense Rumsfield use this example to justify deception.

The Pentagon created a new Office of Strategic Influence under the command of General Simon Worden. Its function included planting false stories in the foreign press.[26] There was an immediate storm of protest.[27] *New York Times* columnist Maureen Dowd asked, "Our cause is just. So why not just tell the truth."[28]

Rumsfeld backed off, leaving the fate of the Office of Strategic Influence to his top lieutenants. He denied he had ever seen the charter for the office.

Was this mendacity?

It was earlier announced at an industry conference that General Worden had briefed Rumsfeld on two occasions and had his basic support; and top Rumsfeld aides confirmed his approval of the broad mission.[29]

The Office of Strategic Influence officially was disbanded, but the Pentagon later awarded a grant to a major defense consultant to study how the Defense Department could design an "effective strategic influence" campaign to combat global terror.

Sound familiar?[30]

THE NO-FLY LIST (FREEDOM TO TRAVEL). "The right to travel is a part of the liberty that was emerging as early as the Magna Carta. . . . Freedom of movement is basic in our scheme of values." *Kent v. Dulles*, 357 U.S. 116 (1958).

In Milwaukee, a Peace Action group planned to fly to Washington to lobby against the School of the Americas in Fort Benning, Georgia (thought to train Latin American military personnel in torture). Sixteen-year-old Alia Kate was the first to arrive. When she went to get a boarding pass she was told to wait. Then a sheriff's deputy came and took her to a nearby building, where she was interrogated at length.

Sister Virgine Lawinger of the Racine Dominicans was also in the group. The lady at the ticket counter told her to wait, and a sheriff's deputy came and took her to an office. She was told her name was "flagged."

Father Bill Brennan of Milwaukee's St. Patrick's Church suffered the same experience. His reaction:

> No one was charged with a crime or threat of crime. No one was advised of his or her civil rights. My personal reaction is fear of the arbitrary use of power this incident reveals. Someone in Washington has the power to inspect a passenger list, discover the motive of our flight (a peace protest) and stop our takeoff.

The scheduled airline waited as long as it could, and then left without the peace group.[31]

Peggy Randall wrote from Hoboken, N.J., that her husband was strip-searched and detained at the Newark airport, missing both his connecting flights, and having his dignity and nerves seriously shaken. Her husband is a United States citizen with an Arab surname.[32]

In San Francisco, Rebecca Gordon and Janet Adams, who publish the *War Times*, were stopped when they attempted to board a flight to Boston. They were questioned by police, and eventually allowed to go their way.[33]

The American Civil Liberties Union filed suit on their behalf to find out why they were stopped. The Transport Security Administration and the FBI at first denied that a "No-Fly" list existed. But a Freedom of Information Act suit revealed that 339 fliers out of San Francisco had been detained (based on the list) since September of 2001, and more across the bay in Berkeley.

The Aviation and Transportation Security Act, signed into law by President Bush on November 19, 2002, creates the office of Transportation Security Administration (TSA). The Act authorizes the TSA to notify air carriers that persons on the passenger list "may be a threat to civil aviation." The air carriers must then "notify appropriate law enforcement agencies and prohibit the individual from boarding an aircraft."[34]

MILITARY TRIBUNALS. "A decent Respect for the Opinions of Mankind" prompted Thomas Jefferson to list the "long string of abuses" behind the Declaration of Independence. One such abuse was transporting citizens "beyond the seas for trial before military tribunals."

On November 13, 2001, President Bush established Military Tribunals to try any of the twenty million noncitizens in the U.S. when the president decides "it is in the interest of the United States that such individual be subject of such order." The court will hold sessions in Guantanamo.

The Bush courts are to be staffed by military personnel especially selected; the courts are to meet behind closed doors; the courts can base their decisions on secret evidence not known to the accused. The accused are denied the Due Process of Law as we treasure it: the right to a "speedy and public trial by an impartial jury," the right to the effective assistance of counsel, the right to be informed "of the nature and cause of the accusation," and "to have compulsory process for obtaining witnesses."[35]

This is not the first time our leaders have turned to special courts. When the witch hysteria hit Salem in 1692, Governor Phips appointed a special court to try the accused, and the court relied on "spectral" or supernatural evidence. The accused were required to recite the Lord's Prayer on the assumption that a "witch," beholden to the Devil, would surely stumble. Nineteen accused were tried this way, found guilty, and hanged. Fifty-six others, in close confinement and under hard interrogation, confessed to practicing witchcraft. Accusations mounted and included Harvard's president Samuel Willard and the governor's wife. It was time to call a halt. Governor Phips dissolved the witch court. The cases were turned over to the regular court for trial in the regular way, and the hysteria subsided. Within five years the colony declared a day of fasting and prayer to atone for the injustice. In 1711 the Legislature gave reparations, and in 1992 the Massachusetts legislature pardoned all the "witches" by name.[36]

During the War of 1812 General Andrew Jackson declared martial law in the city of New Orleans, and limited travel. He arrested Louis Louailler, who wrote in a French-language paper, "It is high time the laws should resume their dominion, that the citizens of this state should return to the full enjoyment of their rights." Jackson charged Louailler with inciting mutiny and disaffection, and confined him under military authority. A federal judge, Dominick Hall, issued a writ of habeas corpus directing Jackson to appear and justify the detention of Louailler. Jackson did not comply. Instead he arrested Judge Hall and confined him in the same prison as Louailler. Finally, news of war's end arrived, and Jackson ended martial law. Judge Hall, back on the bench, ordered Jackson to show cause why he should not be punished for his earlier refusal to respond to the writ issued on behalf of Louailler. After a hearing, the judge held Jackson in contempt, and fined him one thousand dollars. Jackson paid it. Thirty years later, as Jackson lay on his deathbed, Congress remitted the fine.[37]

Abraham Lincoln assumed the presidency faced with a huge rebellion, rebel sympathizers everywhere, and the loyalty of border states like Maryland, Missouri and Kentucky in doubt. The very existence of the nation was at stake. He responded in part with military arrests and suspension of the writ of habeas corpus. He justified his actions when he asked the special session of Congress that met on July 4, 1861, "Are all the laws, but one to go unexecuted, and the government itself to go to pieces, lest that one be violated?"

In September 1862 he issued a proclamation that persons "discouraging volunteer enlistments, resisting military drafts, or guilty of any disloyal practice affording aid and comfort to rebels" should be subject to "martial law and liable to trial and punishment by courts-martial or military commissions."[38]

The military authorities detained some thirteen thousand civilians, and closed a number of newspapers.[37] Matters finally came to a head with the case of *Ex Parte Milligan*, 71 U.S. 2 (1867).

Milligan, a Democrat who lost the race for Governor of Indiana, was a member of the Order of American Knights. There was evidence that Milligan's secret association conspired against the draft, and plotted insurrection, the liberation of eight thousand Confederate prisoners at Camp Douglas, and the seizure of state and national arsenals. They were tried by a military commission, found guilty, and sentenced to death. They petitioned the civil courts for relief, and won. The majority of the Supreme Court held that the Constitution of the United States:

> is a law for rulers and people, equally in war and in peace, and covers with the shield of its protection all classes of men, at all times, and under all circumstances.
>
> No doctrine, involving more pernicious consequences, was ever invented by the wit of man than that any of is provisions can be suspended during any of the great exigencies of government.

The Bush Administration lost sight of this great heritage, the supremacy of the civil over the military. Concern over military tribunals came from far and near—from left and right.

Conservative William Safire wrote that a "panic-stricken attorney general" misadvised the president to replace "the American rule of law with military kangaroo courts." The president's "drumhead tribunals will sit in judgment of noncitizens who the president need only claim 'reason to believe' are members of terrorist organizations." His "kangaroo courts can conceal evidence by citing national security" and "execute the alien" with no review by any civilian court.[40]

Three hundred law professors opposed the military tribunal because it (i) violates the separation of powers, (ii) does not comport with constitutional standards of due process, and (iii) violates binding treaties.[41]

United Nations Human Rights Commissioner Mary Robinson criticized the procedures because, "the right to fair trial must be upheld even in crises."[42]

On July 3, 2003, President Bush designated six captives to be tried before a military tribunal,[43] the members of which were to be chosen by Deputy Secretary of Defense Paul D. Wolfowitz.[44] Two Britons (Moazzam Begg and Feroz Abbasi) and one

Australian (David Hicks) are among the six.[45] Mr. Begg's father in Birmingham, England, was very depressed by the news: "the judge is from the military, the prosecution is from the military, the jury is from the military and even his solicitor is from the military so it is not going to be a fair trial."[46]

After negotiations at top levels[47] the Bush Administration assured the British government it would not seek the death penalty for the two Britons[48] and assured Australia it would not use any secret evidence against Hicks. If convicted, the United States would let Hicks serve his sentence in an Australian prison. American officials said these conditions would apply only to the two Britons and Mr. Hicks, not necessarily to anyone else.[49]

The most recent revisions of the military tribunal authorize the accused to retain civilian counsel. But there are impediments. The civilian defense counsel must have security clearance at the "secret" or higher level; may be kept in the dark about "protected" information; may be excluded from deliberations; must give full time and attention exclusively to the military commission proceeding; must foot the bill out of his own pockets (or those of his client); must perform all research at the site; must agree that the government may monitor confidential attorney-client communications; must disclose to the government any information from his client regarding possible future criminal acts; and must disclose to the prosecution a week before trial all its evidence.[50]

Lawrence Goldman, president of the eleven thousand-member National Association of Criminal Defense Lawyers, would not advise any members to act as civilian counsel at Guantanamo because they would be "lending their legitimacy to what would otherwise be a sham proceeding."

Neal Sonnett of the American Bar Association was troubled about the regulations, especially the one allowing monitoring of conversations. He thought lawyers, by participating in the process, "would lend it an air of legitimacy without being able to contribute effectively" and "we would fall into a trap that lawyers should not fall into." Grant Lattin, an attorney who volunteered to represent the detainees in Guantanamo, thought lawyers should participate but pointed out some practical problems:

> The regulations require defense lawyers to pay for their transportation to and from Guantanamo, the cost for a security clearance can be as much as $2,800, and it would be difficult to devote weeks or months to such a case without compensation.[51]

United States Attorney Mary White has successfully prosecuted twenty-six "jihad" conspirators in a series of open trials in New York City. National Security was not compromised. Why is it necessary to transport persons "beyond the seas for trial before military tribunals"? Did not Jefferson have it right in the Declaration of Independence?

GUANTANAMO (OUR OWN DEVIL'S ISLAND). The Guantanamo base occupies forty-five square miles of Cuba first seized by U.S. forces in 1898 during the Spanish-American War. Since a 1903 agreement the United States has leased the land from Cuba for two thousand gold coins a year, now valued at $4,085. The U.S. government still pays, but Cuban president Fidel Castro refuses to cash the checks.[52]

Officials chose Guantanamo as the site for a prison camp on the theory that it is technically not part of the United States, so constitutional protections would not apply.

Some 660 prisoners captured in Afghanistan are now detained in camp "X-Ray" on Guantanamo Bay on the southern shore of Cuba. Supposedly the captives are Taliban fighters or al-Qaeda terrorists. They come from forty-two different nations—Britain,

Australia, France, Algeria, Yemen, and Pakistan, among them.[53] The prisoners are kept in individual cages eight feet by eight feet with chain-link walls, a floor of slab concrete, and a tin roof. They are allowed out an average of three times a week for twenty-minute periods for a shower and kicking a soccer ball. There is a high rate of attempted suicides, and about one in five of the detainees is being medicated for clinical depression.[54] Vice President Dick Cheney says the conditions are "probably better than they deserve."[55]

A small number of prisoners, judged not to pose a security threat, have been released. Two of the three Afghans released were in their seventies, "wizened old men with canes," partially deaf and unable to answer simple questions. The third, about thirty-five years old, fought with the Taliban but said he had no choice—Taliban solders conscripted him.[56]

The United States plans to release three juveniles[57] and some innocent bystanders captured by Afghan warlords and sold for the bounty offered by Washington for al-Qaeda and Taliban fighters.[58]

Secretary of Defense Rumsfeld plans to hold the bulk of prisoners until the end of the war on terrorism charges—even if tried by a court and acquitted. He says, "To release them after an acquittal so they could return to the battlefield would be mindless."[59]

President Bush has declared that the captives are "unlawful combatants," not "prisoners of war," and that the Geneva Convention does not apply.[60]

The Geneva Convention provides that prisoners of war (i) need only answer questions relating to their name, rank, and serial number; (ii) are entitled to the creature comforts enjoyed by their captors; and (iii) must be released at war's end. It applies to "all cases of declared war or other armed conflict," and includes those in the country's regular armed forces, and those in *irregular forces*, provided they wear identifying insignia and carry arms openly during an attack. If there is doubt, captives must be treated as prisoners of war until their status is determined by a competent tribunal.[61] Secretary of Defense Rumsfeld denies that there is any doubt about these captives' status: "These are bad people" who may have information about future attacks, and "we need to be able to extract from them whatever information they have."[62]

Much of the foreign press thinks the horrors of September 11 have addled America with a "revenge lust that has swept away normal moral concerns."[63]

There is worldwide revulsion to our policy in Guantanamo, and Secretary of State Colin Powell advised the president of "growing complaints from the countries whose nationals are among the prisoners.[64]

Senator John McCain, a onetime prisoner of war, Senator Lindsey Graham, and Senator Maria Centwell visited the detention center and wrote Rumsfeld that it was time either to release the detainees or bring them to trial.[65]

Finally, a suit was filed by twelve detained Kuwaitis and financed by their government (our ally). They allege they are charity workers who were assisting refugees when they were caught up in the war. They were captured by Pakistanis who "sold" them to U.S. troops for the bounty offered for Arab terrorism suspects.[66]

They asked that they be (i) informed of any charges against them, (ii) allowed to meet with lawyers and family members, and (iii) obtain access to an impartial tribunal to review whether any basis exists for their continued detention. The trial judge in the case ruled that the American Naval Base at Guantanamo was not a part of the United States so the court lacked jurisdiction.[67] The Court of Appeals for the District of Columbia agreed that Cuba—not the United States—has sovereignty over Guantanamo Bay and the United States courts "are not open to [the Kuwaitis]."[68]

On November 10, 2003, the Supreme Court agreed to review the issue and decide the jurisdiction of the courts to hear challenges to "the legality of the detention of foreign nationals captured abroad in connection with hostilities and incarcerated at the Guantanamo Bay Naval Base, Cuba." A decision was expected by early summer.[69]

In the meantime the United States Court of Appeals in California disagreed with the Court of Appeals in Washington, D.C., and held that Guantanamo is clearly under the territorial jurisdiction of the United States and thus the plaintiff in a different case, Salim Gherebi, a Libyan, is entitled to the protection of United States law." The D.C. Court went on to say that in times of national emergency, like war, "It is the obligation of the judicial branch to ensure the preservation of our constitutional values and to prevent the executive branch from running roughshod over the rights of citizens and aliens alike."[70]

THE SWEEP (HEARKEN BACK TO THE INTERNMENT OF THE JAPANESE). Twenty-year-old Ould Belal from Mouritania was visiting his cousin in Kentucky. He was arrested, without a warrant signed by a judge, on September 14, 2001, on a false tip that he had taken flying lessons. He was detained in New Albany, Indiana, and then transferred to Bowling Green, Kentucky, then to Memphis, then to the federal detention center in Oakdale, Louisiana. He was released on October 22 on condition he leave the country.[71]

Five young Israeli Jews were arrested on September 11 on the George Washington Bridge leading into Manhattan. They were taking pictures of the smoldering wreckage of the World Trade Center. They spoke a foreign language and seemed to be from the Mideast. They were detained for twenty-seven days in the Metropolitan Detention Center in Brooklyn: "blindfolded during interrogation, handcuffed in confinement." They joined a protest hunger strike sponsored by Pakistani Muslims. They admitted working illegally on tourist visas, and are waiting deportation back to Israel: "Eagerly, friends say."[72]

Abdallah Higazy, a student from Egypt, was temporarily housed in a hotel within eyesight of the Twin Towers. It was evacuated, and a hotel employee found an aviation radio in Higazy's hotel room (or so he said). Higazy was arrested for perjury when he denied it was his radio, denied bond, and confined in isolation. He was not allowed to use the telephone. Under "unrelenting pressure" he admitted he owned the radio and gave three conflicting versions of how he acquired it. He was released when a resident of the hotel, a pilot, complained that his radio was missing.[73]

These are a few of the twelve hundred persons swept up in a frenzy after September 11. Nearly all were immigrants from Arab and Muslim countries. They were held incommunicado, and like the young visitor from Mouritania, moved from pillar to post. Some were kept for months in cells with the lights burning twenty-four hours a day. The Department of Justice's Inspector General Glenn Fine investigated and found videotapes (Detention Center officials told investigator no such tapes existed) showing officers slamming detainees against the wall, twisting their arms and fingers in painful ways, stepping on their leg restraint chains, and keeping them restrained for long periods of time.[74]

Attorney General Ashcroft refused all information about the detainees—who they were, where they were, why they were detained—for their own good, of course. He "respected" their "privacy rights," and feared that a disclosure of identity might create "a public black list."[75] But as criticism mounted, he gave a limited accounting. *Not one of the twelve hundred* swept up after 9/11 had been charged with terrorism or involvement in the September 11 attack.[76] Six hundred were simply let go; 641

were kept in custody on minor criminal charges or violations of immigration laws.[77]

Chief Immigration Judge Michael J. Creppy issued an order that the special immigration cases had to be handled by judges with security clearances, in closed courtrooms with no visitors, no family, no press. The restrictions include neither confirming nor denying such a case is on the docket.[78]

People in the United States should not simply disappear, as they did in Argentina some few years ago. Knowing whom the government has locked up is the necessary first step for public accountability—government with the consent of the governed.

Freedom of Information Act requests were filed to find out if the government acted fairly and lawfully in deportation hearings. On August 26, 2002, the Court of Appeals for the Sixth Circuit (sitting in Detroit) agreed that the executive branch cannot uproot people's lives "outside the public eye and behind a closed door."

The Court of Appeals for the D.C. Circuit ruled the other way. Judge David Sentelle (joined by Judge Karen Henderson) wrote that when government officials tell the court that disclosing the names of detainees will produce harm, "it is abundantly clear that the government's top officials are well suited to make this predictive judgment. Conversely, the judiciary is in an extremely poor position to second-guess government views in the field of national security."

Hopefully the Supreme Court will recognize that "Democracies die behind closed doors."[79]

An earlier "sweep" was led by Attorney General A. Mitchell Palmer after World War I. The Bolsheviks had seized power in Russia. Much of the world was in an uproar. At home, suspected anarchists had set off bombs. Palmer responded with a series of raids. Alleged radicals were rounded up by the thousands, brutalized in local jails, and hundreds of eastern Europeans were deported without due process. Palmer identified the targets of the raids this way: "Out of the sly and crafty eyes of many of them leap cupidity, insanity, and crime; from their lopsided faces, sloping brows, and misshapen features may be recognized the unmistakable criminal type."

The majority of Americans then applauded the Attorney General. The *Washington Post* answered the complaint that civil rights were violated thus: "There is not time to waste on hairsplitting over infringement of liberty."[80]

Today, we consider the Palmer raids illegal, unconstitutional, shameful. History will judge the Ashcroft raids no differently.

MEAN TIMES IN THE LAND. Everyone knows Sherman's remark that "War is Hell." Fewer know about President Woodrow Wilson's despair on the eve of our entry into World War I:

"Once lead this people into war and they'll forget there ever was such a thing as tolerance. To fight you must be brutal and ruthless, and the spirit of ruthless brutality will enter into the very fiber of our national life, infecting Congress, the Courts, the policeman on the beat, the man on the street."[81]

Insecurity and anger can evoke the worst of our instincts. President Bush has authorized the C.I.A to assassinate suspected terrorists, despite a ban ordered by President Gerald Ford and our criticism of Israeli forces similarly targeting Palestinian leaders.[82] Not only assassination, but torture is part of our warfare. We have a secret C.I.A. interrogation center at the Bagram air base in Afghanistan. Suspects are kept in metal shipping containers. Those who refuse to cooperate are kept kneeling for hours in black hoods—at times in awkward, painful positions. They are deprived of sleep with a twenty-four hour bombardment of lights.

In some cases the C.I.A. hands the prisoners over to foreign intelligence services—Jordan, Egypt and Morocco—with a list of questions we want answered. C.I.A. Director George Tenet says interrogations overseas have yielded significant returns.[83]

Maher Arar stopped at JFK airport on his way home to Canada from a business trip in Tunisia. He was detained and sent to Syria, a country he had fled seventeen years before. He was kept in a box, severely beaten, and released after a year of torture because of a public outcry in Canada. The FBI admitted a practice of "rendering" foreign nationals to foreign nations for the purpose of extracting information. Syria admits it held Arar as a favor for the United States.[84]

At home, the President asserts a right to confine American citizens in military prisons—in solitary confinement with no access to counsel, friends or family. The prisoners are to be held time without end, without charges or a chance to defend themselves. It is only necessary to claim they are "enemy combatants." No other president has ever claimed such power.

Critics as well should beware. The White House put a man's wife in danger because he criticized the president. Here's what happened.

In February 2002, Vice President Dick Cheney asked the Central Intelligence Agency to look into claims that Iraq had purchased uranium from the African country of Niger. The C.I.A. asked Joseph Wilson, a former ambassador to Iraq and Gaban, and senior director for African affairs on the National Security Council under President Clinton, to make the investigation. Wilson went to Niger in February 2002 and reported to the C.I.A. and the State Department that the rumor was false and had been discredited for many years. Nevertheless President Bush told Congress (and the world) in his January 2003 State of the Union address that Iraq had obtained nuclear material from Niger.

Mr. Wilson wrote an op-ed piece for the July 6, 2003, New York *Times*, describing his mission, and concluded that intelligence related to the Niger-Iraq uranium transaction had been twisted by the White House to exaggerate the Iraq threat. Within a week "senior administrative officials" "leaked" to conservative columnist Robert Novak that Wilson's wife, Valerie Plame, was a C.I.A. operative on "weapons of mass destruction." Novak published this in his syndicated column on July 14. On July 22 two journalists for *Newsday* reported they had been told that Plame worked in an "undercover capacity."

It is illegal for any official with access to classified information to disclose the identity of a covert American agent. The C.I.A. requested the Department of Justice to begin a criminal investigation into who was behind the leak. On September 30, the Department of Justice announced its investigation of the White House.[85]

Mr. Wilson charged that Karl Rove, the president's top political advisor, had leaked the story, or at a minimum condoned the leak.[86] Wilson said the leak about his wife "wasn't to intimidate me, because I'd already said my piece. This was to keep others from stepping forward."[87]

Attorney General John Ashcroft has close personal ties to Karl Rove and ultimately took himself out of the investigation.[88] A special counsel, Patrick J. Fitzgerald, the United States attorney in Chicago, was appointed to lead the investigation, which at this writing was still in progress.[89]

On another occasion Ashcroft testified before the Senate Judicial Committee that critics of the administration were "aiding terrorists by providing ammunition to America's enemies." Saying he was speaking to "those who scare peace-loving people with phantoms of lost liberty, my message is this: your tactics only aid terrorists."[90]

Justice Brandeis once noted that our government, "for good or evil teaches the whole people by its example. If the government becomes a law breaker, it breeds contempt for the law; it invites every man to become a law unto himself."[91] With or without encouragement from on high, home-born terrorists fire-bombed mosques in Dallas, San Francisco, Alexandria, Virginia, and Dearborn, Michigan.[92]

In Ohio, mosques were bombed in Columbus, Toledo, and Porma.[93] From Texas to Chicago to Long Island came reports of arson, personal attacks, and police arrest of men in Middle Eastern head gear.[94]

Janis Heaphy, the publisher of the Sacramento *Bee*, gave the graduation speech at the California State University in Sacramento. She promised to be brief (ten minutes) but was hooted off the stage before that.

She urged the audience of ten thousand to safeguard their rights of free speech. The audience booed.

She wondered what would happen if racial profiling became routine. The audience cheered.

She asserted that the Constitution makes it our right to challenge government policies. Clapping, chanting, and heckling forced her from the podium.

A university vice president recalls that, "it was when she started defending habeas corpus that things went down hill."[95]

Down the road a bit, there was a free speech issue at Berkeley. The University of California houses the Emma Goldman Papers Project, named for the anarchist deported to Russia after World War I. In a fundraising letter the curator used two of Goldman's quotes. The first, from a 1915 speech, called on people "not yet overcome by war madness to raise their voice of protest." The other, from a 1902 speech, warned that free speech advocates "shall soon be obligated to meet in cellars, or in darkened rooms, and speak in whispers." University officials ordered that the two quotations be deleted, lest they be construed as a political statement by the University in opposition to U.S. policy toward Iraq.[96] After a storm of e-mail protests, Chancellor Beardahl decided to let the quotations stay.[97]

The Dixie Chicks fared less well. Lead singer Natalie Maines told a London audience, "we're ashamed the president of the United States is from Texas." Clear Channel Communications, owner of some twelve hundred U.S. radio stations, then pulled the Dixie Chicks from their stations' play lists. The trio, meanwhile, said their lives and the lives of their families had been threatened in the aftermath of Maines's London comment.[98]

So it goes. Actor-director Tim Robbins was disinvited to the Baseball Hall of Fame for speaking out against the war. His wife, the actress Susan Sarandon, was disinvited by the United Way of Tampa for her anti-war comments. First Lady Laura Bush disinvited a distinguished group of American poets from a White House conference on "Poetry and the American Voice." Some had planned to read anti-war poetry, and the poet laureate of Connecticut planned to wear a silk scarf with peace symbols. What, asks poetress Katha Pollitt, "is the White House afraid of, poems and scarves?" [99]

Benjamin Franklin said long ago: "They that can give up essential liberty to obtain a little temporary safety deserve neither liberty nor safety."

We have a long history, going back to the Alien and Sedition Acts of 1798, of jettisoning our civil liberties when our security seems threatened. We look back on each situation with remorse, but repeat the error when the next crisis comes along. So it is today. And this too will pass. But can we park our hard-earned liberties on a shelf somewhere for the duration of a crisis and not expect them to be moth-eaten and crumbled around the edge when the crisis ends? The sound and fury of the Bush war on terror will be for naught if in the end we find we have destroyed the very freedoms for which we fought.

In the United States, the "home of the brave," we must in the words of Martin Luther King, "hew out of the mountain of despair a stone of hope." We must, all of us, take alarm at the many incursions upon our liberties, and lift high our voice of protest. As freeborn Americans we can do no other.

Truth and the Bill of Rights are the early victims of wartime hysteria—from the prosecution of Jeffersonian editors under the Alien and Sedition Acts in the 1790s to the Spanish-American War (Remember the Maine!), and on to the internment of Japanese-Americans in World War II. Today, the Bush Administration wants to tap our phones, punish dissenters, and hold aliens and citizens alike indefinitely in close confinement without charges, without counsel, without a trial.

How unlike the example set by North Carolina Governor Jeb Vance during the Civil War.

There were large desertions after Bull Run, and the Confederate forces made a sweep through North Carolina rounding up able-bodied men of draft age. They were detained in military prison on suspicion of desertion, all without the right to be heard. Vance wrote Confederacy president Jefferson Davis to go slow in suspending the writ of habeas corpus and threatened to recall North Carolina troops from the front lines to uphold the principles of "Anglo-Saxon liberty." The proudest boast of his governorship, he later wrote, was that the "laws were heard amidst the roar of the cannon." ∎

The Intolerable Burden

Connie Curry

For the past ten years, I have been savoring the second gift of my life—writing about some of the people that I met during the civil rights movement of the 1960s. The first gift was to be part of that movement, starting with the Student Nonviolent Coordinating Committee from its founding in 1960 until 1964, and then for eleven years as the Southern field representative of the American Friends Service Committee, wandering around the South, following the wonderful tenet of the Quakers—"Proceed as way opens."

My recent work on books and a documentary film about the people and issues of the movement has driven home to me both the astonishing gains that were achieved in the Sixties but also the extent to which those gains are now threatened and have already been eroded.

Southerners—indeed all Americans—need to wake up to the resegregation of our schools, to the linkage between poor segregated schools and prison incarceration rates, to the increasing view by some of prisons as an industrial segment of the economy, to the unconscionable disparity of incarceration rates between majority and minority populations, and to the vast and growing disfranchisement of significant percentages of minority men. No one who digs into these issues can avoid seeing the correlations between them.

Unfortunately, in today's partisan climate, these conditions actually benefit the politics of wealth and privilege while handicapping the politics of openness and equality.

Some background is in order.

After the passage of the 1964 Civil Rights Act, of which Title VI mandated a plan for school desegregation, many Southern schools, particularly in rural areas, submitted a "freedom of choice" plan to Washington. This scheme theoretically allowed all parents to send their children to the school of their choice. The white power structure knew full well that black parents, trapped in most Southern states in the economic peonage of the sharecropping system, would not dare choose a white school for their children.

However, there were black families who faced the challenge in every Southern state, and it was my pleasure and honor to meet and try to assist several of these "ordinary" people who were willing to make the choice and face the consequences. From 1965–75, I worked closely with the Carter family of Sunflower County, Mississippi. Matthew and Mae Bertha Carter had thirteen children and sharecropped on a cotton plantation not far from Drew, Mississippi, in the heart of the Delta. Drew is a few miles from Parchman Penitentiary, a few miles from Ruleville, home of Fannie Lou Hamer, and not far from Senator James Eastland's 5,800-acre cotton plantation in Doddsville. Right outside Drew, the remnants

---

Author and activist CONNIE CURRY was a founding member of the Southern Non-violent Coordinating Committee (SNCC) and later was the Southern field representative of the American Friends Service Committee. In recent years she has explored the unfinished business of the 1960s through books (*Silver Rights*; *The Fire Ever Burning*; *Deep in Our Hearts: Nine White Women in the Freedom Movement*; and *Mississippi Harmony*) and a documentary film, *The Intolerable Burden*. She lives in Atlanta.

of a barn mark the site where Emmett Till was lynched in 1955 for allegedly whistling at a white woman.

The first five Carter children graduated from the ill-equipped "colored" school and left home immediately to join the military or to find jobs outside of the state. Mae Bertha and Matthew were determined to get a better education for the rest of their children, filled out the "freedom of choice" forms, and in the fall of 1965, sent their seven school-age children to the previously all-white schools in Drew. For five years, the Carter children remained the only blacks in these schools and were subjected to insults, harassment and humiliation until the courts ordered full desegregation in 1970. That suit, filed by Marian Wright Edelman and others with the NAACP Legal Defense and Educational Fund in Jackson, asked for injunctive relief against the operation of a racially segregated system that placed a "cruel and intolerable burden" on black pupils and parents.

In the meantime, the Carter house was shot into, their crops were plowed under, their credit was cut off, they were evicted from the plantation, and they could not find jobs for some time. Finally, with the help of the AFSC and other groups they were able to find a house in Drew, jobs with Head Start, and better treatment in general when the powers in Drew realized that the Carter family had support from the outside world. I lost track of the Carters in 1975 when I left AFSC and went to work for the Atlanta city government, but I ran into Mae Bertha in 1988 at the King Center when she attended a conference on Women in the Civil Rights Movement.

We hugged each other and in answer to my question about the family she told me that Matthew had died earlier that year, the children, including Carl (the baby in 1965) had graduated from the Drew High School, all eight had gone on to college, and seven had graduated from Ole Miss. I realized then that I wanted to tell their story, and *Silver Rights* was published in 1996. Subsequently, Aaron Henry, an even better-known Mississippi civil rights leader, read the book and asked me to help tell his story; *The Fire Ever Burning* was published in 2000. That same year, I wrote a chapter in and edited *Deep in Our Hearts: Nine White Women in the Freedom Movement.* In 1994, at the thirtieth anniversary celebration of the 1964 Mississippi Freedom Summer, Bob Moses had encouraged us all to tell our own stories so that history might be more accurate. Thus in 2002, *Mississippi Harmony* was published. And I collaborated with Mrs. Winson Hudson of Leake County, Mississippi, to finish her memoirs.

After *Silver Rights* was published, several people asked Mae Bertha to tell her story on video and film, and what an experience to watch! Her humor, vitality, and courage come shining through, and Chea Prince, an associate in Atlanta, urged me to do a documentary on the Carters.

With his help as director and editor, we finished *The Intolerable Burden* in spring 2003, and it subsequently won the American Historical Association's John O'Connor Award for outstanding interpretations of history through film or video.

We began with the idea of telling the Carter story and showing the success the Carter children had made of their lives. We interviewed all eight of them. Beverly, who desegregated A. W. James Elementary school as the lone third grader, cries as she tells of having no one to play with—ever, standing alone against the school wall during play period, watching the little white girls jump rope, wishing that she could jump. We interviewed white people from Drew, some who had attended school with the Carters and who now regret their ignorance of what was taking place or their silence if they did know. Other whites remain adamant today in their belief that the civil rights movement ruined "the Southern way of life." The headmistress of the all-white private Sunflower

Academy told us the history of its establishment, and the assistant school superintendent spoke of the high dropout, expulsion, and suspension rates in the now mostly black Drew High School. Senator Willie Simmons, the first black state senator from the Delta since Reconstruction, decried the enormous state allocations for prisons/corrections instead of state support of education.

As Chea and I developed the story, we realized that we needed to look at it through the eyes of Mae Bertha. She passed away in 1999, a fighter for justice until she drew her last breath. We knew she would want us to tell the whole and continuing story—the total picture. Thus, the film is divided into three parts, segregation, desegregation, and resegregation. There is a fourth step, however: incarceration.

Our film ends with an epilogue, "Education vs. Incarceration," and points out that the Sunflower County pattern of failing public education for blacks and minorities, and poor people in general, and the fast track to prison is being replicated throughout the United States. It is sobering indeed to see in the epilogue that one of Mae Bertha's grandchildren, Lorenzo, son of one of the older Carter men, raised by his maternal grandmother in Drew, is serving a long term in Parchman Penitentiary for dealing drugs. The film reflects the dismal conditions of these poor rural towns like Drew, with zero tolerance policies in the schools, no jobs, no industry, and deserted streets. One young black man says in the documentary—"can't go to school, no jobs, no way to get to the next nearest town to work—nothing to do but get caught up in the street life."

The reactions to the documentary have been a revelation. We have shown it in venues from Ithaca, N.Y., to Harvard, from South Carolina to California, to AFSC groups, universities, history associations, high schools, and a corporate diversity training group. One pervasive reaction is the general lack of knowledge of the civil rights movement and the conditions that prompted the struggle of the 1960s. This was, after all, only forty years ago—we are not talking about ancient Roman history here. The lack of historical knowledge comes mostly from younger people, but surprise at the treatment of the family and the lives of blacks in general is expressed often by adult audiences from outside the South.

The film is generally accepted with warmth and enthusiasm by black audiences, and I have noticed tears on people's faces who have approached afterwards and told me that it brought back their own experience as the first black child in a white school in Tallahassee, Florida, or Florence, South Carolina, or Richmond, Virginia, to name a few examples. In one mostly white audience, I was told that it was too depressing and why couldn't I just end with the Carters all graduating from Ole Miss? Why talk about prisons?

In an all-black high school in Jackson, Mississippi, the students cheered when Mae Bertha Carter says it's useless to be afraid to die—that you are already dead if you let people control your lives. Many black activists respond to the film saying that just having children in integrated schools won't ever make any difference as long as the curriculum is geared to a white world and how success or achievement is measured in that world. Little by little people are recognizing the reverberations of "resegregation" in their own communities, where those who can afford it (mostly white) are sending their children to private academies. And they talk of "desegregated" schools, where segregation occurs by stealth in honor programs or advanced placement classes which are almost always majority white. We are continuing to create a better-educated white elite.

Almost all audiences have been surprised at the direct connection between the failure of public education and the fast track to prison for youth of color. They are quite willing to admit that the issue of education versus incarceration exists everywhere and to acknowledge how much money is being spent on building prisons and keeping them filled. They are stunned, however, to learn that with more than two million people in prison, the United States has the world's highest incarceration rate. If you add those on probation and parole, the figure is 6.5 million or one in every 32 adults. The majority of U.S. inmates are black males, but prison populations are increasingly inclusive of Hispanic, other minorities, and poor people in general. The elements of racism and discrimination cover a broad spectrum ranging from police profiling to disproportionate death penalty convictions. In between are the issues of prison privatization, mandatory sentencing, lack of indigent defense, prison sentences instead of drug treatment, abominable prison conditions, and lack of reentry or aftercare programs.

My own civil rights orientation makes me perhaps most outraged over statistics concerning felony disfranchisement. More than 4.6 million Americans—or 2 percent of the voting-age population—are barred from voting because of past criminal convictions (even if they have completely served their sentences and are not on probation or parole). Because more than 60 percent of the prison population is black or Latino, the voting power of these groups is disproportionately diluted.

On a nationwide basis, one in eight African American males is denied the right to vote. This translates to about 1.4 million black men. The number of Hispanic voters similarly disfranchised is approaching 15 percent. Whose interest does this serve? Depriving convicted felons of the vote is done on a state-by-state basis and the method for reinstatement varies. There is movement in several states to do away with these laws. As Mae Bertha Carter used to say in an irate voice, "People died so black people could vote."

Looking at the larger picture, particularly in the South, we are reaping the whirlwind from policies planted thirty years ago. We have been surrounded by messages of "get tough on crime," "three strikes and you're out," mandatory sentencing, disparities in drug sentencing between crack and cocaine, and media portrayals of "young black predators." Most Southern states now spend more on incarceration than on education, and George Bush's application of the underfunded "Leave No Child Behind" program takes a great toll on children who don't test well, and feeds them right into the school-to-prison pipeline. Also under Bush and the Republicans, private prisons are springing up, often in rural areas where people are duped into believing that the prisons will improve their economies, and people are traded on Wall Street instead of off a slave block in Charleston, South Carolina.

Year before last, NAACP national board member Clayola Brown from New York and some colleagues were visiting various towns and facilities near Jackson, Mississippi. They were standing outside a prison and were approached by a young black boy who told them he was nine years old. He pointed at the prison and told them that is where he wanted to go—that he had heard from his friends that you could get three hots and a cot, that it was warm in the winter and cool in the summer, running water all the time, and had new books because you could go to school in there. He thought that maybe, because they "looked like him," they might be able to get him in.

These public education and criminal justice injustices, hidden and ignored, have spread from the South to infect much of present-day America. Remedying these ills must become the cutting edge of the human rights movement in this country. ■

A Postcard from Norway: How America Looks from Here

Charles Bussey

Born in Oxford, Mississippi, I have lived nearly sixty years in Kentucky where I teach American History at Western Kentucky University. Currently I am in Kristiansand, Norway, teaching a course called "The American South" as a Fulbright Scholar. This program was inaugurated in 1946 with legislation sponsored by Arkansas Senator J. William Fulbright to create better understanding between the United States and foreign nations. In that sense, my wife Donna and I view ourselves as missionaries in a mission field in a 2004 world where the United States is viewed through many eyes as a rogue nation. It has been my purpose to demonstrate by word and deed that not all Americans, especially those of us from the American South, are arrogant and without international sensibility.

It is a fertile field, for I have discovered that among most Norwegians, including faculty and students at my university here, as well as ordinary citizens in the Kristiansand community, there is a strong anti-American feeling. By that I mean anti-American government—not anti toward American individuals. In fact, Donna and I have been extended many acts of kindness. We had been told by many people not to expect much of Norwegians beyond common courtesy and a friendly smile. Certainly, we were informed, you won't be invited into homes and you won't be taken into the confidence of those you meet. For the first week or two here in Kristiansand, that was true. Then we heard one of my colleagues, a poet named Annabelle Despard, speak to the international students at Agder University College. After going through a delightful introduction to Norsk culture and ways that Norwegians think and act, and in response to a question of how foreigners should act in Norway, Annabelle concluded by saying, "In the end, just do what your heart tells you." Being very outgoing, I took that to heart—as did my less-outgoing wife.

We had heard a lot about the Setesdal Valley near Kristiansand toward the mountains where there is an isolated knitting museum near Telemark where a famous World War II raid against the Germans was conducted by Norwegian resistance fighters. I wanted to go, so I talked to one of my students, a fifty-four-year-old grandmother named Inger, and asked if she might help us figure out how to get up the valley to Ose and the museum. She thought about it briefly and said, "I will take you there in my car. I will arrange everything."

Two weeks later we set out. It was a lovely day in September, and Inger had brought a picnic lunch of homemade bread smeared with blue cheese and a thermos of coffee. Three hours later we were in Ose and introduced to Annemor, a well-known expert who often lectured in the U.S. about Norwegian sweaters and knitting techniques. Five minutes later we were off with Inger and Annemor along the Otra River to pick Norwegian tyttebaer for jam. Later, we toured Annemor's shop and the museum. Following

---

CHARLES BUSSEY is a professor of history at Western Kentucky University. During the writing of this essay, he was a Fulbright Professor at Agder University College in Kristiansand, Norway, where he taught "The American South" and "America: 1950-1975."

that we enjoyed a delicious fresh whole trout dinner with potatoes, vegetables, and wine in the old and tiny Ose Hotel which had maybe four rooms upstairs and a dining room that seated fifteen at the most. That night we sat in the basement of Annemor's shop drinking wine and chattering away like old friends about politics in America, especially about President George W. Bush, the Iraq War, and the direction America was taking under his leadership. Both Inger and Annemor were well informed. In addition, Annemor regaled us with stories about her most recent lecturing experiences in the Seattle area. Her hosts there for several weeks were leaders in the Green Party and in the American movement to simplify life styles. She thought it particularly amusing that one Seattle attorney's idea of simplifying his life style meant going from twenty suits to ten. We all laughed as we sat in a very primitive building in Norway's Setesdal Valley!

Inger and Annemor reminded me of American Southerners with their concern about the distinctiveness of place, of people, and of belonging. They talked of common acquaintances, where they lived, what they did, and naturally they concluded finally that they were distant kin. By 11 P.M., Donna and I were ready for bed, and Annemor said that she planned to row home across the fjord since she'd been drinking wine and didn't want to drive. She showed us where we were to sleep—upstairs above her shop in a bedroom separated from Inger's room by a common sitting area—and we settled in. The next morning, we discovered that Annemor and Inger had talked far into the night, but that Annemor had come back early and fixed us a huge breakfast with fresh baked bread from her basement oven which accommodates forty loaves at a time. She served us the usual assortment of meats, cheeses, and jams—but also fresh green beans from the garden, uncooked! It was the best of Southern hospitality, in "southern" Norway.

From Norway, looking back toward the United States, it is

somewhat easier to put the current American government and its action in historical perspective. The American South, unlike the Norwegian South, was built on an arrogance and violence that revolved around first slavery and then segregation, and it is clear that America today, led by George W. Bush, has "moved" south. America now seems to have undergone a "Southernization" process and become the worst of the South, to have drifted far to the right politically and socially. "Are we all Kentucky now?" I thought to myself the other night watching BBC World news. By that I mean, Kentucky currently has two right-wing Senators and a right-wing governor, and Kentuckians express far too often the intolerant, provincial and repressive ideas of the radical religious right. People in my home state of nearly sixty years now seem to have no shame that the United States is violating the Constitution as well as international law in its use of power. I wonder if Norwegians are different from Americans or whether Norway just lacks the overwhelming power which America possesses. While I think that there is a basic human nature common to all people, there does seem to be a gentleness, a sense of international responsibility, and a respect for the rights of others among Norwegians that is lacking among many Americans. Perhaps that is merely a reflection of historical circumstance, a question of power, a matter of social construction. Still, it does give one pause.

I have taken the opportunity of being a Fulbright Scholar in Norway to reread several times Senator Fulbright's 1966 book, *The Arrogance of Power*. Based on lectures he delivered at Johns Hopkins University in 1964, and published two years later in large measure as a response to America's rush into madness in Vietnam, it is an amazing book to read almost four decades later. He wrote, for example, "America is now at that historical point at which a great nation is in danger of losing its perspective on what exactly is within the realm of its power and what is beyond it. Other great nations," he said, "reaching this critical juncture, have aspired to too much and, by over extension of effort, have declined and then fallen. Gradually but unmistakably America is showing signs of that arrogance of power which has afflicted, weakened, and in some cases destroyed great nations in the past."

Reading those words in Norway in 2004 jolted me. The U.S. today is clearly dominated by an arrogance of power, and "we are not living up to our capacity and promise as a civilized example for the world." Fulbright reminds us that "the measure of our falling short is the measure of the patriot's duty of dissent." It is clear that the more things change, the more they stay the same. Presidents who engage in warring, in misleading the American people as they take us to war, in violating international agreements and the Constitution, know no party boundaries. Fulbright, himself a Democrat, was responding to a Democratic president (LBJ) and a Democratic Congress taking us to disaster in Vietnam while today it is a Republican president and a Republican Congress which has us on the verge of calamity. In thinking about this, it crossed my mind that the only American president in my living memory who might have avoided, who might have taken a different tack, was Jimmy Carter—a Southerner, who only recently was in Norway to receive the Nobel Peace Prize. While Carter made mistakes, he understood the difference between hope/memory and optimism/nostalgia. Most important, however, he understood that greatness has more to do with relationships and service than it has to do with power and prominence.

Carter, a Southern Baptist, took his religion seriously and demonstrated that his was a living faith in the best of the Southern religious tradition, and that too reminds me of southern Norway. Kristiansand, I was told shortly after my arrival here, is "the Bible Belt of Norway." It's true. In addition to the regular Norwegian State Church (Lutheran), there are innumerable Protestant offshoots, free churches, and Pentecostal groups. It's like being at home! Carter, unlike President Bush, learned from his religion that there are human limits, and he tried to teach the nation that lesson, though he seems to have failed.

President Bush sees no limits. Never has an American president invoked the name of God more often nor I believe in such fundamentally flawed ways as George W. Bush. His references are usually connected to statements identifying the United States as God's chosen country and with America carrying out God's mission. While this construct is not unique to Bush—we heard it all in the mid-1840s when the term Manifest Destiny, the God-given right of white America to take the whole continent of North America from Atlantic to Pacific no matter who already controlled the land—it is amazing to hear it revived. Does history teach us nothing? The most blatant or excessive comment the President made came three days after 9/11 when he spoke at the National Cathedral in Washington, D.C., and said, with no qualification, it is America's "responsibility to history" to "rid the world of evil." It astounds me that an American president—after slavery, the Cold War, Vietnam—would be that thoughtless. Such pride—saying that America could do what God has not done—flies in the face of Bush's claim to be Christian.

Living in Norway, where BBC World is our source of world news, Donna and I realize that Americans may be the only people in the world who believe the rhetoric of America's president. Norwegians certainly don't. Especially not Christians. For example, one day a student came up to me after class and identified herself this way: "I am a devout Christian. How could anyone read the New Testament, the words of Jesus, and act like your president?" She was not attacking me personally—she likes me—but she was just so puzzled. Norwegians, like most Scandinavians, think that Americans are simple, that they see politics and world events without nuances, and they especially believe this about President Bush and his advisors.

This brings me back to Senator Fulbright and how he might have advised our current president. "We are not," Fulbright wrote, "God's chosen savior of mankind but only one of mankind's more successful and fortunate branches, endowed by our Creator with the same capacity for good and evil, no more or less, than the rest of humanity." Since coming into office, and in the shadow of 9/11, President Bush has radically transformed himself and the direction of the United States. From talking about humility and international cooperation before 9/11, Bush has rapidly moved America toward becoming one of the most arrogant nations in history. I believe that is because we are so powerful, and "power tends to confuse itself," as Fulbright pointed out in 1966, "with virtue, and a great nation is peculiarly susceptible to the idea that its power is a sign of God's favor." Confederate soldiers thought that God was on their side in the American Civil War. I wish that President Bush would take a few moments to read Fulbright's book and note the words, "Who are the self-appointed emissaries of God who have wrought so much violence in the world? They are men with doctrines, men of faith and idealism, men who confuse power with virtue...."

The prayer that keeps playing in my head, "War Prayer," comes from Mark Twain: "O Lord our God, help us to tear their soldiers to bloody shreds.... Help us to turn them out roofless with their little children to wander... the wastes of their desolated land.... We ask it, in the spirit of love, of Him Who is the source of love." While many people would agree that taking out Saddam was beneficial, President George Bush believes that Saddam's removal represents God's will.

We are clearly today involved in a misadventure, and it is always difficult to extract oneself from that once it's started. History is littered with stories of nations and leaders who found it impossible to stop policies once in place even when advised by people close to them that such a path was destructive. America's own LBJ found this out in Vietnam. Senator Fulbright knew that when he wrote in 1966, "We may be thinking about how disagreeable it would be to accept a solution short of victory; we may be thinking about how our pride would be injured if we settled for less than we set out to achieve; we may be thinking about our reputation as a great power, fearing that a compromise settlement would shame us before the world. . . ." When my students here ask, "Why can't America just recognize her mistakes?," I read them that passage.

The concept of American Exceptionalism mentioned earlier in this essay had its genesis in John Winthrop's 1631 sermon, "A Model of Christian Charity," delivered aboard the ship *Arabella* before the English Puritans disembarked in Salem, Massachusetts. Winthrop talked about establishing a "city upon a hill," a model of Christian community for the rest of the world to follow. Many American politicians have used this phrase, and some have embellished it. President Ronald Reagan, for example, inserted the word "shining" before city. What Reagan seems not to have known or remembered if he did know it is that the city on a hill was conditional, not divine. That city, according to Winthrop, was constantly under God's judgment and would collapse if it proved false to its promise. Like Reagan before him, George Bush often uses America as an example to the world. On September 11, 2002, he said: "This ideal of America is the hope of all mankind. . . . That hope still lights our way. And the light shines in the darkness. And the darkness has not overcome it." That quotation came, of course, from the New Testament, but the writer (John) was talking about God's Word, about Christ, not America! Reagan maybe, but certainly Bush, confuses the American Civil Religion with Christianity and borders on blasphemy.

I don't doubt that President Bush's faith is sincerely held, but thinking Americans must be concerned as to how his faith impacts both foreign and domestic policies. While my focus in this brief essay has been on the Administration's warring, let there be no mistake, military violence abroad is intimately connected to domestic policies and especially those related to poverty. A wise man once said, there is a "connection between war and poverty. . . . Poverty is militarism's twin." This administration is using the Iraq misadventure to cloak its war on social programs at home. Instead of LBJ's "war on poverty," we seem now to be engaged in a war on the poor.

Recently retired Kentucky physician and former state senator N. Z. Kafoglis wrote to me:

> The Bush administration is the most dangerous administration in many decades. It launched a preemptive war on the flimsiest evidence that there was an imminent threat to our country. It has cut taxes while incurring the greatest deficit in our history. . . . It has alienated much of the world which used to respect us. . . . Administrative policies are even more hypocritical when it comes to the environment. . . . Funding for student loans has been cut, and we have lost [two and one half] million jobs in the past two years while the President keeps saying things are getting better. For anyone who might objectively assess the administration's record, the conclusion would have to be that it has no credibility.

While the failure to deal with the health care crisis in America, where forty to fifty million Americans are without protection, is horrendous, the most callous example of this "war on the poor" comes with the Bush administration's effort to destroy Head Start. Often criticized after its inception in 1965, this program gradually came to have widespread bipartisan support by the 1990s. It was (is) a program designed to give a hand up to those children in America who grow up in poverty. Who, for God's sake, would want to gut Head Start? The answer is clear—those who seem to despise the poor and hate government and government programs (unless they are military). Unlike attacks on other social and environmental programs, however, there is still a political necessity to cloak attacks on children as "reform." Bush uses such phrases as "leave no child behind" and "school readiness" to disguise the efforts of his administration to dismantle Head Start, which owes much of its success to people like Julius Richmond, the founding director, and Leslie Dunbar, who supported Head Start from the Field Foundation. Both men fought early on to protect and maintain Head Start in the face of efforts from the political right in America to destroy it. The Bush plan, with its narrow focus on literacy, would completely compromise the original intent of Head Start to approach disadvantaged children with a comprehensive program emphasizing both physical and mental health, prenatal care, dental health, nutrition, decent housing, parent training, and access to other social services that impact a child's current and future ability to succeed in school and life.

President Franklin D. Roosevelt once said, "Let us not be afraid to help each other—let us not forget that government is ourselves and not an alien power over us." Those words have no meaning for Bush and his ideological handlers who want to destroy the social services remaining from the New Deal and the Great Society. FDR's words bring me right back to Senator Fulbright who said, "In the abstract we celebrate freedom of opinion as part of our patriotic liturgy; it is only when some Americans exercise it that other Americans are shocked." Remember the Bush-Cheney-Rumsfeld litany "if you're not with us, you're against us." Rubbish! They're radicals, they're un-American, they're anti-democrats! As Fulbright said, "To criticize one's country is to do it a service and pay it a compliment." For "in a democracy dissent is an act of faith...." Continuing, he wrote, "criticism ... is more than a right; it's an act of patriotism, a higher form of patriotism, I believe, than the familiar rituals of national adulation." We in America are in the process of becoming what we despise—a rogue nation. The White House published in September 2002 a "National Security Strategy" which is so reminiscent of NSC-68, a 1950 document from the National Security Council which provided the strategy and framework for the Cold War. That earlier document led inescapably to the terrible cost of militarism at the expense of social programs and to Vietnam. The White House candidly admits that the Bush strategy represents a major shift in military strategy, maybe the biggest in fifty years, but who cares? America is the world's cop, the only superpower, and might makes right.

Secretary of Defense Rumsfeld, the primary architect of the new strategy, surely knows that it represents a radical reorientation of the political character of America. It indicates that the United States can act alone, anytime and anyplace, and can act in preemptive fashion against anyone the president determines to be terrorist. This would mean, Kentucky author Wendell Berry wrote, that "The law in the world, then, is to be upheld by a nation that has declared itself above the law."

Scandinavia, committed firmly to international cooperation, generally is skeptical of the policies developed by George W. Bush and his key advisors. The Danish Crown Prince in a recent interview with a French magazine used the word "simple" in an unflattering way to characterize American foreign policy. That reinforces the Norwegian idea which Donna and I often encounter that America's aim to "rule" the world presumes too much, is childish. Keep in mind that Norway, with fewer than five million inhabitants and independent only since 1905, clearly recognizes that she has little international clout. Norway has, however, found a niche as an international peace maker and has created the International Peace Research Institute in Oslo.

Donna and I spend considerable time with Helge and Trine-Lise, a retired M.D. (nephrologist) and secretary respectively. In their mid-sixties, both are taking my class "The American South," but the four of us gather often to eat and to talk about art and literature—as well as American politics and policy. Born in Norway in 1936, Helge spent his youth between ages eight and eighteen in Westchester County, New York, and New Jersey. His father, a Norwegian resistance fighter, fled to the United States when the occupying German forces discovered his work, and found employment in the United States with Norwegian shipping interests. After his father died, Helge returned to Norway and became a doctor. This couple, with enormous affection for America and her *ideals* of justice, freedom and equality, is disenchanted with America's current international policy.

The Norwegian way in short is clearly not the Bush way of "my country right or wrong," or "America, love it or leave it," and which is based on the premise that America is all "good" and those who oppose the U.S. are all "evil."

Senator Fulbright's book, which I have quoted several times, appeared in 1966. A year later, breaking with the Johnson administration's Vietnam policy, Martin Luther King preached a powerful sermon on April 4, 1967, at Riverside Church in New York City. King brilliantly distinguished nationalism—"if you're not with us you're against us"—from patriotism. "We are at the moment," King said, "when our lives must be placed on the line if our nation is to survive its own folly. Every man [and woman] of humane conviction must decide on the protest that best suits his [or her] conviction, but we must all protest." As King put it that day, "We can no longer afford to worship the god of hate or bow down before the altar of retaliation. The oceans of history are made turbulent by the ever-rising tides of hate. History is cluttered with the wreckage of nations and individuals that pursued this self-defeating path of hate."

King's eloquent plea reminds me of today, when my nation again seems "trapped" in the senseless occupation of a nation which poses no threat of imminent danger to the United States. America is a strong and wealthy nation, and my dream is that someday—soon I hope—we will have leadership which will focus our resources and energy on making peace rather than war.

Clearly, warring as a result of arrogance is not confined to Republican President George W. Bush. As indicated earlier, it doesn't take a long memory to recall Democrat Lyndon Johnson and his party's ill-fated efforts in Vietnam. We lost more fifty thousand people there, to say nothing of the untold numbers of Vietnamese killed, and we wasted significant sums of money. Maybe no American president is immune to an arrogance of power. I don't know.

What I do know—as Fulbright taught us—is that it is the responsibility of American citizens to rise up and say NO MORE. Berry said, "If we are serious about peace, then we must work for it as ardently, seriously, continuously, carefully and bravely as our government now . . . [wages] war." That brings me back to the class I am teaching in Norway—"The American South." My Norwegian students in the class love the Southern Civil Rights Movement. So do I. That movement taught us that love is more powerful than hate, that nonviolence can beat violence, and that the powerless in America can bring those in power to their knees. President Bush, who constantly uses Christian imagery, should pay attention to the historical Southern Civil Rights Movement and the words of Jesus who taught: "Blessed are the meek, for they will inherit the earth. . . . Blessed are the merciful, for they will receive mercy. . . . Blessed are the peacemakers, for they will be called children of God." We need today in the United States nothing less than the resurrection of the Southern Civil Rights Movement in all its splendor.

For my part, I am proud to be a dissenting Fulbrighter, a Southerner, and an American. ∎

Democracy Cannot Be Exported If It Is Not Secure at Home

Laughlin McDonald

Amid growing concern over the curtailment of civil liberties at home and American unilateralism and imperialism abroad in the wake of the war on terrorism, the discussion over extending an essential part of the 1965 Voting Rights Act has understandably been muted. But if the key provision is allowed to expire as scheduled in 2007, the result could be the significant erosion of black voting power in the Southern states. Were that to happen, the hypocrisy of America's professed crusade to establish democratic principles of inclusion and self-determination abroad would become intolerable.

At issue is Section 5 of the Act, which requires most jurisdictions in the South to get prior federal approval of changes in their voting procedures.

Speaking during an earlier extension debate, C. Vann Woodward, the dean of Southern historians, warned Congress in 1981 of the consequences of failure to extend Section 5. "I do think it reasonable," he told a House committee, "to warn that a weakening of . . . the preclearance clause will open the door to a rush of measures to abridge, diminish, and dilute if not emasculate the power of the black vote in Southern states. Previous testimony before your committee has shown how persistent and effective such efforts have been even with the preclearance law in effect. Remove that law and the permissiveness will likely become irresistible—in spite of promises to the contrary. . . . I hope that retreat from the Second Reconstruction will not make it necessary for some future generation to face a Third."[1]

Congress listened carefully to Woodward, as well as others who testified before it, and extended Section 5 in 1982 for an additional twenty-five years, the longest extension in the Act's history. As the Senate report concluded: "There is virtual unanimity among those who have studied the record that Section 5 preclearance should be extended. . . . Continued progress toward equal opportunity in the electoral process will be halted if we abandon the Act's crucial safeguards now. . . . Without the preclearance of new laws, many of the advances of the past decade could be wiped out overnight with new schemes and devices."[2]

Those who study the record today, as opposed to theorizing about color-blindness, will similarly conclude that Section 5 preclearance should again be extended. Much progress has indeed been made in minority voting rights and office holding in recent times, but it has been made in large measure *because of* the existence of Section 5 and the other provisions of the Voting Rights Act. One of the principal conclusions of *Quiet Revolution in the South* (1994), the most comprehensive study of the impact of the Act to date, was that "Quite simply, had there been no federal intervention in the redistricting process in the South, it is unlikely that most Southern states would have ceased their practice of diluting the

---

LAUGHLIN MCDONALD is director of the Voting Rights Project of the ACLU. He has represented minorities in numerous voting and other cases, testified frequently before Congress, and has written extensively for scholarly and popular publications on constitutional and civil liberties issues. His most recent book is *A Voting Rights Odyssey: Black Enfranchisement in Georgia.*

black vote."[3] The fact that Section 5 has been so successful is one of the arguments in favor of its extension, not its demise.

What has been going on in Georgia in recent years is an enlightening case study which shows that the reactionary temptation to manipulate the law in ways that will disadvantage minority voters is as irresistible today as it has ever been. The State of Georgia's brief in *Georgia v. Ashcroft* (2003) provides a vivid, modern-day example of its willingness to roll back the protection the Voting Rights Act gives to minorities.

As we know, minority voting at the local level has been vital in reshaping the South after the Civil Rights Movement. And as we saw in Florida in 2000, local impediments to minority voting can have profound national implications.

The issue in *Georgia v. Ashcroft* was whether the district court properly denied preclearance under Section 5 to three of the state's proposed new senate districts drawn after the 2000 census. Under the new plan, compared to the pre-existing plan, the "Black Voting Age Population" in Senate District 2 had been reduced from 60.58 percent to 50.31 percent, in Senate District 12 from 55.43 percent to 50.66 percent, and in Senate District 26 from 62.45 percent to 50.8 percent. The Black Voting Age Population had actually been reduced in twelve of the majority-black districts, but only in three did the district court conclude that the state failed to carry its burden of proof that the reductions were not "retrogressive," or did not diminish the electoral opportunities of black voters. The Black Voting Age Population had also been reduced in a number of House districts. The district court, however, precleared the entire House plan, noting that there was no evidence "that might suggest that these decreases will have a retrogressive effect."[4]

The Supreme Court vacated the decision and sent it back to the district court for further review. Far more important to minority voting rights than whether the three reconfigured districts are ultimately found to be retrogressive was the state's repetition of the old arguments, a demonstration of the continuing disdain many Southern politicians have for the Voting Rights Act, and their willingness to subordinate the interests of minority voters to partisan concerns. Little has changed in their arguments or their attitudes in forty years, only in the degree of their influence.

Georgia had argued against passage of the original Voting Rights Act in 1965. Assistant Attorney General Paul Rodgers, Jr. testified before a Senate committee that under the proposed bill covered states "could not longer [sic] adopt legislation on their own." The bill was "a yoke of disgrace" and its provisions were "very unjust."[5] Carl Sanders, the Democratic governor, wrote directly to President Lyndon Johnson and urged defeat of the pending bill. It was "an extreme measure," Sanders said, and moreover it was not needed because the state had enacted a "modern" election code in June 1964, "which provides sweeping safeguards for guaranteeing and inspiring exercise of the elective franchise."[6] Congress discounted these objections and passed the Voting Rights Act by substantial majorities in both houses. Georgia's response was immediately to join a suit brought by South Carolina in which it argued, unsuccessfully, that the Voting Rights Act was unconstitutional.

When extension of Section 5 was debated in Congress five years later in 1969, Georgia's then governor, Lester Maddox, and its attorney general, Arthur Bolton, led the fight against the proposed legislation. Maddox testified before the Senate that "[t]he Voting Rights Act is illegal, unconstitutional and ungodly and un-American and wrong against the good people in this country. . . . And phooey on anything that says otherwise."[7] Bolton was more restrained in his commentary than the governor, but he advised the Senate subcommittee in a letter that "it will come as no great shock to you to discover that my office is not overly fond of Section 5 of the Voting Rights Act of 1965."[8] Not all Georgians were opposed.

Vernon Jordan, the black director of the Voter Education Project in Atlanta, anticipating the warnings issued by C. Vann Woodward in 1981, said that Georgia and other Southern states "that were the most efficient, determined, and malicious in their efforts to keep black people off the registration rolls can be expected to be the most efficient, determined, and malicious in their efforts to cancel out the growing black vote." Particularly in rural areas, he said, "hundreds of . . . Southern communities stand poised and ready to eliminate the burgeoning black vote."[9]

Congress, citing the continued depressed levels of black voter registration and the significant noncompliance with Section 5 by the covered jurisdictions, voted to extend the special coverage provisions of the Act for another five years. It concluded that extension "is essential . . . in order to safeguard the gains in Negro voter registration thus far achieved, and to prevent future infringements of voting rights based on race or color."[10]

Georgia's 1971 congressional reapportionment—the first such reapportionment subject to Section 5 review—showed both the wisdom of congressional extension of the preclearance provision and the extraordinary lengths to which the legislature was prepared to go to exclude blacks from the congressional delegation. The state's two African-American state senators, Leroy Johnson and Horace Ward, both of whom were elected from majority black districts, proposed a plan in which the fifth congressional district took in the city of Atlanta, and increased its black population from 34 percent to 45 percent. The plan was defeated in the Senate by a vote of 43 to 9.

The plan that was finally adopted discriminated in three distinct ways. First, it divided the concentration of black population in the metropolitan Atlanta area into three districts to ensure that district five would be heavily majority white. Second, it excluded from the fifth district the residences of two prominent blacks who were known to be potential candidates, Andrew Young and Maynard Jackson. Third, to maximize the chances of white control, the residences of whites who were recognized as potential candidates were included in the district bounds. Rep. G. D. Adams of Atlanta made clear his reasons for supporting a district that limited the black population: it was to ensure the election of "a white, moderate, Democratic Congressman."[11] When the plan was submitted for preclearance, the attorney general objected because he was unable to conclude "that these new boundaries will not have a discriminatory racial effect on voting by minimizing or diluting black voting strength in the Atlanta area."[12]

Under the duress of Section 5, the state enacted a new plan increasing the black percentage in the fifth congressional district to a near majority. At the ensuing election in 1972, Andrew Young won the fifth district seat and became the first black elected to Congress from Georgia since Reconstruction.

The white leadership of the state essentially boycotted the 1975 congressional hearings on the next extension of Section 5. Attorney General Bolton, in response to a letter from the U.S. Senate subcommittee requesting a written statement of the state's position on the proposed amendment, wrote a terse and chilly letter that "[a]s Attorney General for the State of Georgia in a number of litigated cases my position with respect to the law in this matter is well established, and I do not at this time have anything further to add."[13] In one of the cases Bolton litigated, the state had argued that the Voting Rights Act was unconstitutional. Andrew Young, however, the only black member of Georgia's congressional delegation, testified in support of the extension of Section 5. Echoing Vernon Jordan, and again anticipating C. Vann Woodward, he cautioned that "it would be extremely dangerous to all of the progress we have made thus far if we did not keep that section very active in the bill."[14]

Congress extended Section 5 in 1975 for an additional seven years, concluding that the past experience of evading the Voting Rights Act by covered jurisdictions "ought not be ignored in terms of assessing the future need for the Act." It was "imperative," according to the Senate report, that Section 5 protection apply to the redistricting that would take place after the 1980 census.[15] Congressional prescience would once again be fully vindicated by subsequent events.

A federal court denied preclearance to Georgia's congressional plan adopted after the 1980 census concluding that the state had again deliberately minimized the black population in the fifth congressional district to avoid drawing a majority minority district and had applied different standards depending on whether a particular community was black or white. In defending its refusal to draw a majority black district in the Atlanta area, the state made arguments which "color blind" conservatives and the Supreme Court would later seize upon to justify the destruction of majority minority districts and to challenge race-conscious affirmative action at every level. A majority black district, state legislators said, would "bring out resegregation ... in a fine city like Atlanta," would cause "white flight," would disrupt the "harmonious working relationship between the races," and would be simply a "ghetto district" with no real political power.[16] The federal court, however, found that these reasons were entirely pretextual. Joe Mack Wilson, chair of the House reapportionment committee and the person who dominated the redistricting process in the lower chamber, explained to his colleagues on numerous occasions that the real reason for minimizing the black population in the fifth district was—in his words—to keep from drawing "nigger districts."[17]

Oblivious to the racism inherent in the state's political process, white officials continued their assault on the Voting Rights Act and Section 5. In testimony before the Senate in 1982, Freeman

Leverett, a former assistant attorney general of Georgia who had defended the state's infamous county unit system two decades earlier in the Supreme Court, said that the Voting Rights Act had been passed in 1965 "to appease the surging mob in the street." Section 5 should be repealed, he said, because "there is no longer any justification for it at all."[18] The city attorney for Rome, Robert Brinson, expressed his "distaste" for Section 5 and argued that the statute should be allowed to expire. Other witnesses from Georgia, including some of its most respected civil rights leaders—Rev. Ralph Abernathy, Julian Bond, Ed Brown, and Rev. Joseph Lowery—testified in support of the amendments.[19]

In extending Section 5 in 1982 for a record twenty-five years, Congress took special note of the efforts in Georgia to circumvent minority voting rights, including non-compliance with Section 5, the switch by counties from district to at-large elections, and the adoption of the discriminatory congressional redistricting plan.

Georgia's 1990 redistricting was embroiled in Section 5 objections and lengthy "backlash" litigation brought by the state's increasingly conservative white majority, who convinced an increasingly conservative Supreme Court that placing whites in majority black districts could be a form of reverse discrimination. After the smoke of the litigation had cleared, one of the state's congressional districts, ten of its senate districts, and thirty of its house districts remained majority black.

The majority-minority districts drawn in the South in the wake of the Voting Rights Act, far from being discriminatory or segregated, were actually the most racially integrated districts in the country, containing an average of 45 percent of non-black voters.[20] Integrated majority-minority districts have not only not balkanized society, but have in fact dampened racial bloc voting and, according to one analyst, promoted a "politics of commonality."[21] Frank Parker, a respected civil rights lawyer with extensive experience in voting rights litigation, has further concluded that "the creation of majority-minority districts and the subsequent election of minority candidates reduces white fear and harmful stereotyping of minority candidates, ameliorates the racial balkanization of American society, and promotes a political system in which race does not matter as much as it did."[22] Highly integrated majority-minority districts, despite the self-serving claims of proponents of "color blindness" that they cause resegregation, are the surest path to meaningful biracial politics in the South.

It is obvious that the Voting Rights Act has worked, and despite constant attack from Southern conservatives, continues to work. But the Old South fights on, and its influence has grown.

In its brief in *Georgia v. Ashcroft* filed in March 2003, the state resurrected its anti-Voting Rights Act, states' rights rhetoric from prior years and argued that Section 5 "is an extraordinary transgression of the normal prerogatives of the states." Because of federal intervention, state legislatures were "stripped of their authority to change electoral laws in any regard until they first obtain federal sanction." The statute was "extraordinarily harsh," and "intrudes upon basic principles of federalism." As construed by the district court, the state said, the statute was "unconstitutional."[23] But the arguments the state advanced on the merits were far more hostile to minority voting rights than its states' rights rhetoric.

One of Georgia's principle contentions was that the retrogression standard of Section 5 should be abolished in favor of a coin toss, or an "equal opportunity" to elect, standard based on Section 2 of the Voting Rights, which it defined as "a 50-50 chance of electing a candidate of choice." It made the further, and utterly irresponsible, argument that minorities—the very group protected by the Act—should be totally excluded from participating in the Section 5 preclearance process. The Supreme Court rejected the state's invitation to rewrite Section 5, as well as its attempt to deny minorities a voice in Section 5 preclearance.[24]

Georgia argued further that "the point of equal opportunity is 44.3 percent Black Voting Age Population, which means that 'there's a 50-50 chance of electing a candidate of choice' in a district with an open seat and with 44.3 percent Black Voting Age Population."[25] The adoption of Georgia's standard for an equal opportunity would have permitted the state to abolish *all* of its majority black districts. While whites would have been able to control the outcome in the overwhelming majority of districts in the state, black voters would have been able to elect only half of the candidates of their choice—and as a practical matter far less than that—in the so-called "equal opportunity" districts. Given the tendency of blacks to vote Democratic, white Democrats would have been the obvious beneficiaries of such a scheme (and black Democrats the losers), and blacks would have been turned essentially into second-class voters. They could elect candidates of their choice, but only if the candidates were white. One court has likened such an electoral scheme to the comment attributed to Henry Ford that "[a]ny customer can have a car painted any color he wants so long as it is black."[26]

Georgia is not the only covered state to make such arguments. The Democratic governor of South Carolina argued in a post-2000 census case involving court ordered redistricting in South Carolina that a Black Voting Age Population as low as 45.58 percent was the "point of equal opportunity," and was all the Voting Rights Act required in the way of protecting the rights of minority voters. The federal court, in a carefully reasoned opinion, rejected the argument and concluded that "a majority-minority or very near majority-minority voting age population in each district remains a minimum requirement" in order the satisfy the requirements of the Voting Rights Act.[27]

On the eve of passage of the Voting Rights Act, there were

fewer than a hundred black elected officials in the entire eleven states of the old Confederacy. By January 1993, the number had grown to 4,924. The key to the increase in effective minority political participation and black office holding has been the creation of majority-minority districts under the protection of the Voting Rights Act.

Throughout the 1970s and 1980s, only about one percent of majority white districts in the South elected a black to a state legislature. As late as 1988, no black had ever been elected from a majority white district in Alabama, Arkansas, Louisiana, Mississippi, or South Carolina. The number of blacks elected to state legislatures increased after the 1990 redistricting, but again the gain resulted from an increase in the number of majority black districts.

The pattern of blacks winning almost exclusively from majority black legislative districts is particularly evident in Georgia. Of the ten blacks elected to the state Senate in 2002, all were elected from majority black districts. Of the 38 blacks elected to the state House, 35 were elected from majority black districts. Of the three who were elected from majority white districts, two were long term incumbents while the third was elected from a three-seat district.

Given the continuing levels of white bloc voting, white candidates are prohibitive favorites to win in most majority white legislative districts in Georgia, and indeed throughout the South. Abolishing majority black districts, or providing black voters an opportunity to elect candidates of their choice only in districts with reduced black populations that provided a 50-50 chance of losing, would cause a significant reduction in the number of black office holders. The advocacy of such positions by Georgia and South Carolina, and their attempts to implement them, are by themselves compelling reasons Section 5 must be extended.

The interests of minority voters are plainly not adequately protected by Southern states which advocate the abolition of majority-minority districts, the subordination of the interests of minority voters to partisanship, and the exclusion of minorities from the preclearance process. And minority interests are not protected by the current wave of national politicians who have embraced the Old South view that Section 5 of the Voting Rights Act should simply disappear. There will surely be an assault on the Voting Rights Act when this issue arises in Congress in the months ahead. Now is the time for minority voters and their allies to prepare for the ensuing struggle.

Just as the United States could not fight Nazi racism in Europe during the 1940s and continue to tolerate a Jim Crow system at home, we cannot pretend to export democratic principles abroad if we do not insure full and equal political participation by racial minorities in our own country. The extension of the special preclearance provisions of the Voting Rights Act is essential if we are to maintain America as a nation where the promise of an inclusive society is also the reality. Black and white voters alike need the Voting Rights Act. We would be foolish to entrust our voting rights—described by the Supreme Court more than one hundred years ago as "preservative of all rights"[28]—to biased and manipulative Southern politicians, especially those who have reached the national stage. ■

Identity Politics, Southern Style

Sheldon Hackney

"THERE HAS BEEN MUCH talk about the politics of identity," writes Henry Louis Gates, Jr., "a politics that has a collective identity at its core. One is to assert oneself in the political arena as a woman, a homosexual, a Jew, a person of color.... The politics of identity starts with the assertion of a collective allegiance. It says: This is who we are, make room for us, accommodate our special needs, confer recognition upon what is distinctive about us. It is about the priority of difference, and while it is not, by itself, undesirable, it is—by itself—dangerously inadequate."[1]

Jean Elshtain has written compellingly of democracy as the working out of self-limiting freedom and of the current impediments to a healthy deliberative democracy. Among her worries is the rise of identity politics. She writes:

> Rather than negotiating the complexity of public and private identities, those who adopt this view disdain and displace any distinction between the citizen and whatever else a person may be—male or female, heterosexual or homosexual, black or white. One seeks full public recognition as a person with a handicap or a particular sexual orientation, or membership in an ethnic or racial group, and exhausts one's public concerns. Marks of difference, once they gain public recognition in this form, translate all too easily into group triumphalism as the story grows that the public world is a world of many I's who form a we only with

others exactly like themselves. No recognition of commonality is forthcoming. We are stuck in what the philosopher calls a world of "incommensurability," a world in which we literally cannot understand one another.[2]

With conservatives gleefully shouting encouragement from the Amen Corner, the sorts of intellectuals formerly known as "liberals" squirm uncomfortably in the grasp of their identity-group allies from the Sixties. Arthur Schlesinger, Jr., who is not a right-wing fanatic, has worried at length about the threat of tribalism.[3] Todd Gitlin, a veteran of Sixties activism and a sympathetic critic of the tattered, postmodern remnants of the American Left, argues tellingly that multiculturalism in general, and identity politics in particular, inhibits and weakens the Left by precluding any notion or vocabulary of the common good.[4] One could easily multiply such examples. All decent Americans apparently abhor identity politics.

"Identity politics" is a subcategory of multiculturalism, and both of those terms have diverse meanings. In some usages, identity politics refers to any social transaction in which a person's group identity plays a part—and that is just about all social transactions. "The personal is political," ran the slogan from the women's movement in the Sixties. "Accused of politicizing everything," Todd Gitlin writes, "identity politics responds that politics is already ~~everywhere; that interes~~ts dress up as truth but are only interests; Alabama native SHELDON HACKNEY is Professor of History at the University of Pennsylvania with special interests in the history of the South since the Civil War, the 1960s, and the American identity. He has served two universities—Tulane and Penn—as president, and he was chairman of the National Endowment for the Humanities during the Clinton Administration. Hackney is the author of *Populism to Progressivism in Alabama*, *The Politics of Presidential Appointment*, and other books.

that power is already everywhere and the only question is who is going to have it."⁵

Here, however, I wish to focus more narrowly on the role of cultural identity groups in electoral politics. Further, I wish to grapple with an apparent contradiction. As David Hollinger noted in *Postethnic America*, "the United States is endowed with a *non*ethnic ideology of the nation"; yet "it is possessed by a predominantly *ethnic* history. . . ."⁶ Similarly, George Frederickson observed in his presidential address to the Organization of American Historians in 1998, "Group membership may be produced by shared historical experiences and social status and not by genes or cultural essences, but ethnoracial identity provides a locus from which most Americans view the world and is a major determinant of whom they vote for, hire or promote, associate with, and welcome as neighbors."⁷

We excoriate identity politics in theory, but we embrace it in practice. In the real world, politicians and pundits, consultants and analysts, Right as well as Left, practice their crafts in terms of identity groups. For instance, we were told frequently during the 2002 midterm elections that the Democratic strategy was to produce as large a turnout as possible among black Americans, while the Republican strategy was to excite their base, especially the religious right. A glance at the exit poll results confirms that the professionals knew what they were talking about, and that the Republicans did a superior job.

Exit polls from the presidential election of 2000 make the same point in a more reliable way because turnout was higher. Al Gore won the popular vote, but George W. Bush carried the Supreme Court. For present purposes, the interesting thing is that the close vote was not evenly distributed across all social groups. The South, black and white together, was the most Republican section of the country (55 percent). Whites who described themselves as members of the "religious right" gave 80 percent of their vote to Bush, while African Americans were 90 percent in favor of Gore. Jews nationally cast Democratic ballots at a rate of 79 percent, as did Hispanic voters at the level of 62 percent, while Southern whites were 65 percent for the Republican candidate.

There was also a huge gender gap in the 2000 election. Bush attracted 60 percent of the male vote. While women in the aggregate were very evenly divided, those who pursued careers outside the home were decidedly in Gore's camp, while those who worked as homemakers were for Bush. This is "family values" at work in the polling place.

If one is tempted to conclude that the South is so heavily Republican because it is characterized by features that predict Republican votes throughout the country, such as Protestant Christianity or rural residence, one must also come to terms with the fact that the South has disproportionate numbers of people at lower levels of education and income, which are powerful predictors nationally of Democratic votes. It is impossible not to conclude that Southern voters are being moved by factors that are peculiar to the region. It is also prompts us to think of white Southerners as an identity group, just like African Americans.

Identity group politics is traditional in the United States. Historians of nineteenth century America have understood for some time that identity group solidarity explained much more electoral behavior than other quantifiable variables. Industrial labor was frequently organized in ethnic federations, and the New York City ethnically balanced ticket is a running joke in political circles.

One of my favorite cartoons from the 1960s is by Jules Feiffer. It contains eight panels, each one a drawing of LBJ's head. The President is speaking:

> First, the Negroes revolted. Then the Puerto Ricans revolted. Then the youth revolted. Then the intellectuals revolted.

In order to preserve law and order, I have had to put them all in jail.

But punitive measures are *not enough*. These troubled times cry out for new answers to unsolved *old* problems.

To seek out the *causes* of anarchy and propose a *cure* I have this day appointed a *fact finding commission*.

To this commission I am appointing

1 Democrat

1 Republican

1 Young Person

1 Old Person

1 Intellectual

1 Anti-intellectual

1 Negro

1 Bigot

Come Let Us Reason Together.

When Bill Clinton in the 1992 presidential campaign deliberately criticized Sister Souljah for her defense of "gangster rap" lyrics that seemed to condone the murder of white policemen by black youth, he was practicing a kind of identity politics. He was distancing himself from the white-fright stereotype of the black community; he was repositioning his party in the minds of suburban whites who viewed the Democratic Party as the sponsor of racial and ethnic minorities, and the promoter of countercultural values. When George W. Bush speaks to a crowd in south Texas or Florida in Spanish, he is practicing identity politics; his subtext is that the Republican Party is not hostile to the aspirations of the Hispanic community. When Pat Buchanan exhorted a Mississippi audience in the 1996 primary campaign not to let "them" take America away from "us," the divide among identity groups was clear.

Is this disjunction between what we do and what we profess

merely hypocrisy? The question is interestingly complex. In his comparative study of race in the United States, South Africa, and Brazil, Anthony Marx notes that almost everyone in Brazil notices that poverty increases as skin color darkens. Yet, no one, not even poor blacks, attributes the poverty to racism. Marx's explanation is that Brazil differs from the United States and South Africa in that the state (the government) never acted to construct or define race as a legal category. When the state codifies racial identity, he argues, it perpetuates racial categories as significant social realities that facilitate discrimination against the group that is being marginalized. Ironically, the resulting racial solidarity is also useful to the oppressed group when it mobilizes to liberate itself from racial oppression.[8]

This certainly fits the American case. Much of the meaning of being African American has been in the process of legal construction and constant revision since the seventeenth century. It has been constantly contested, of course, and it has changed dramatically over time, but the identity is rooted in the law and in a conflictual relationship with the Euro-American majority. The national Republican Party in the late nineteenth century gave Southern whites their way over race relations in order to knit the white nation back together after the Civil War and Reconstruction. The exclusion of blacks was the mechanism for the fusion of whites.

The race-baiting used against white racial liberals in the South was a way of suppressing dissent, and it had the added benefit of reinforcing the Southern white identity. Just as patriotism can be invoked to silence those who seem to oppose the nation when it is acting as the nation, race baiting worked in the South because the white Southern identity was originally and fundamentally a racial construction. This helps to explain the weakness of white liberals. They were marginalized at home, and they were also vulnerable to pressures from the cosmopolitan North where they desperately wanted acceptance and support. They were cosmopolitans living in a parochial culture.

There was some important white support for the Civil Rights Movement when it assumed the guise of a mass movement in the 1950s and 1960s, but the Second Reconstruction was most importantly a mobilization of black communities and black institutions to abolish the legally defined disabilities of race. Those black institutions and the black consciousness of African American communities had been made necessary by the legal strictures of segregation. Small wonder that African Americans see identity politics as a natural extension of interest-group politics.

Euro-Americans outside the South see things differently. Perhaps this is because, since the advent of "Black Power" in 1966, and the onset of the "ethnic chic" revival of the 1970s, identities of difference have for the first time in the twentieth century been asserted from below. Before the 1960s, despite the existence of theories of pluralism and myths of equalitarian assimilation—melting pot and mosaic—the single model available in the public arena for new Americans or excluded Americans was Anglo-dominance. It held that if you look and act and speak like old-stock Euro-Americans, you can blend in and be accepted. The stranglehold of Anglo-dominance was broken by the social justice movements of the 1960s. The new racial and ethnic equalitarian orthodoxy was represented in the Civil Rights Act of 1964, the Voting Rights Act of 1965, and the Immigration Act of 1965. The new dispensation blossomed in an increase in individual possibilities, a multiplication of legitimate models in almost every area of life. Consensus came to seem repressive. Aside from the familiar irony of teenage conformity to nonconforming modes of dress and behavior, standards of any kind became somewhat suspect.

We are still trying to find some accommodation to the Sixties, some way of adjusting our ways of living and thinking to the new social realities, or some way to turn back the tide of change. The current "culture wars" are largely symbolic battles about the multicultural national identity that has its roots in the Sixties. Reacting to the failure of the Senate to convict President Clinton, and distraught about the remarkably robust levels of public approval of the impeached president, Paul Weyrich, head of the Free Congress Foundation and hard-right moral crusader, announced to his constituents that the conservatives had "probably lost the culture war."[9] As welcome as that result might be, the ultimate outcome is actually not at all clear. It is clear, however, that there is widespread worry among the public about social fragmentation, the growing social, physical, economic, and cultural separation of Americans from each other. That worry is exacerbated by identity politics.

It is easy to recognize why black Southerners might view identity politics as a natural mode of promoting self-interest; the attitude of Southern whites takes a little thought. It is undoubtedly somehow linked to the cultural filter through which Southern whites view reality. If, as George Tindall invited us to do twenty-five years ago, we think of Southern whites as an ethnic group,[10] then the question becomes, "Why does the Southern white ethnic identity exert such a hold on its members? Why is Southern whiteness "unmeltable?"

Southern white identity was created out of conflict with the North. It was a social construction invented to fashion a consciousness of commonality among whites living in a slave society and therefore affected by the antislavery movement. Common African ancestry existed before "race" was "constructed" in the seventeenth century as a category that would permit slavery. Similarly, Southern whites shared the fact that they lived in a slave society before the abolitionist movement (whatever time you pick for the origins of that movement at a significant level), but it was that movement that created a consciousness of commonality because it was perceived by whites as a threat. Thus was invented a mythological people whose mission was to protect a besieged social order. This reading is true whether you think of slavery simply as an economic system or as a way of ordering a biracial society.

We know the history of this new identity group. Secession, defeat, Reconstruction experienced as revolutionary tyranny, the creation of the myth of the Lost Cause as a counterweight to New South apostasy, reconciliation with the white North at the expense of black Southerners, the creation of the Solid South in response to the threat of Populist political insurgency, the disfranchisement of blacks and the creation of a social order based upon racial segregation at the turn of the twentieth century, continuing white poverty that was interpreted as more oppression at the hands of the industrialized North, the rise to covert national power of the political leaders of the white Southern identity group between 1938 and 1968 in coalition with non-Southern Republicans, the undermining of that "system" by the Civil Rights Movement and the Voting Rights Act of 1965, and then the flight of Southern whites to the suburbs and to the GOP. The white South has been the most significant locus of dissent in American history.

Paradoxically, the South has been intolerant of internal dissent. Though there is a tradition of dissent within the white South—anti-secession, white Republicanism, Populism, racial liberalism, labor unionism, civil rights sympathizers, even the rumor of a Communist here and there—the region has been as heterodoxically starved as it has been economically poor by comparison with the rest of America, making Southern white dissenters even more heroic than they otherwise would be.[11]

There is an explanation for that. The comparative scarcity of white dissenters in the nineteenth century South may derive from the simpler social structure of a dispersed agricultural society. That society contained fewer non-geographical nooks and crannies where dissenters could achieve some insulation from a disapproving social order. It was a more homogeneous society with fewer elements of conflicting interests, and therefore fewer groups with the functional freedom to develop discordant beliefs.

Add to this the thought that American individualism in its nineteenth century incubator justified itself in terms of the welfare of the whole community. Greedy, self-centered, atomistic, solipsistic individualism was not the American ideal. As Robert Wiebe has put it, "Free individuals formed democratic communities; democratic communities sustained free individuals."[12] This explains why Alexis de Tocqueville observed both rampant American individualism AND an energetic associational life, and why Frederick Jackson Turner saw the frontier as both the birthplace of American individualism AND of a barn-raising, corn-shucking cooperative ethos.

As David Potter long ago pointed out, the nature of individualism changed as the conditions of society shifted from the nineteenth to the twentieth centuries. In the nineteenth century, self-reliant individualism was in vogue because society needed people who could take care of themselves as they pushed their way across the continent or built an industrial economy. As the specialized roles of urban, industrialized life replaced self-sufficient farmers and independent craftsmen in the twentieth century, and as society needed independent action less and independent thinking more, individualism began to mean intellectual nonconformity or dissent. The sin of the nonconforming individualist, of course, is that he undermines the ability of the community to protect its values and self-image against the criticism or assault of outsiders. The community cannot tolerate that, especially a community like the white South that sees itself as besieged by alien forces.[13]

The South lived in the nineteenth century more thoroughly and longer than did the non-South. The result is the persistence of the sort of self-reliant individualism that acts to protect the community from nonconformity. Add to that the notion that the Southern white identity is the product of a series of perceived threats, and one can understand why confrontations with the "cultural other" will revivify the sense of crisis and reinforce parochial conformity. Parochial white Southerners experience a loss of liberty when the freedom of their group is threatened, whether the threat comes from the Civil Rights Movement, the counterculture, the federal government, or some phantasmagoric combination of the three.

If Dan Carter is right, as I think he is, about George Wallace being the precursor to the Republican ascendancy in Washington (the New Republicans), the meaning of the South in a curious sense has become the meaning of America. Or, at least, that is what is at issue in the present political battles. We should not miss the irony of the unintended consequences of black enfranchisement by the Voting Rights Act of 1965. In 1972, the South was solid once more, but it was not Democratic.

Many have noticed the remarkable prominence of Southern political leaders recently. During President Clinton's second term, the President, Vice President, Speaker of the House and Majority Leader of the Senate were all from the South. When Newt Gingrich of Georgia self-destructed, he was replaced briefly by Robert Livingston of Louisiana, who was quickly discovered to have the same problem of not living according to family values. Then, the Republicans were apparently reluctant to have as the picture of their party the next two most senior possibilities, Phil Gramm and Tom DeLay, both Texans, and both like Gingrich carpetbaggers and fugitives from the academy. Dennis Hastert breaks the Southern hold on national leadership, unless you are among those who believe that he is the mouthpiece of Tom DeLay, the Republican majority leader.

When Senator Trent Lott in December 2002 heaped praise upon retiring Senator Strom Thurmond, and ventured the opinion that the nation would have been better off if Thurmond and the

Dixiecrats had won in 1948, he was allowed to twist gently in the politically correct breeze before being eased out of the way so Senator Bill Frist of Tennessee could take his place as Majority Leader.

Thurmond's own place in the pantheon of Lost Cause heroes was put in jeopardy when, after his death in 2002, his daughter from a relationship between the young Strom and the even younger black maid in the Thurmond household, came forward in public for the first time. It wasn't that this sort of thing had never happened before, it was simply the monumental hypocrisy of it all. The prominence of Florida in the 2000 election, and of so many Southern politicians among the leaders of both parties, is not necessarily evidence of the natural superiority of Southern politicians.[14] It undoubtedly says a lot about the importance of the South to the electoral strategies of both parties. It is a battleground region.

Meanwhile, back in the Clinton administration, six of the thirteen House managers of the impeachment trial were white Southern men, and they were an extremely visible six. In contrast, their initial five-person witness list of people from the enemy camp "looked like America" (Monica Lewinsky, Sidney Blumenthal, Betty Currie, Vernon Jordan, and John Podesta)—two Jews, two blacks, two women, and one Greek/Italian hybrid. This tableau dramatizes Dan Carter's thesis that George Corley Wallace was the founding father of the New Republican Majority; he lead the Southern white ethnic revolt against the federal government and against the party of big government because those two entities had been sponsors of the Civil Rights Movement and of various other "out groups," opposition to which helped to define the Southern white identity.[15] Southern white ethnic animosities happened to coincide with the animosities of the stalwart core of the New Republicans: the cultural conservatives and the religious right.

Now, the reason identity politics arouses such suspicion is that it confounds the American belief in the liberty of self-definition. We are told by our culture that we can construct ourselves, and reconstruct ourselves. We can choose our own values and even our own identities. Even if we recognize ontological difficulties with this notion, and even if we believe that race is a "social construction," it is not for the most part an individual option, despite the clear lesson of Thurmond's biracial family. Identity politics is thus at war with a central feature of the American identity. Ironically, of course, it has been the denial of access to this self-determining, self-choosing realm of society that has caused some Americans to resort to identity politics in the first place.

If this is a fair abstract of a version of Southern political history and of the Southern white identity, several interesting implications leap out. First, of course, Southern whites have been playing identity-group politics since the abolitionists first raised their voices, and they have been particularly active in recent years. That blacks and other minority groups were coming under fire for practicing just the sort of identity group politics that has been traditional in the South is fundamentally unfair.

Second, surveying regional history since the Missouri Compromise in 1820, we must conclude that while the content or meaning of racial categories frequently changes, the categories themselves persist. They persist and they continue to shape, though not determine, the history of the region and its people.

Third, cultural identity is stronger as a political force than is economic self-interest. A long line of Southern liberals and sympathetic observers has operated on the assumption that the South could not be redeemed until race was somehow taken out of politics. That "somehow" was generally thought to be by a politics of economic self-interest that would bring together blacks and whites in a biracial coalition of the poor.[16] That was the road not taken in the Populist revolt of the 1890s or in the New Deal.

In this tradition, Bob Dylan sang in 1963 about the murder of Medgar Evers:

> A Southern politician preaches to the poor white man,
> "You got more than the blacks, don't complain.
> You're better than them, you been born with white skin,"
> they explain.
> And the Negro's name is used, it is plain
> For the politician's gain, as he rises to fame
> And the poor white remains
> On the caboose of the train
> But it ain't him to blame
> He's only a pawn in their game.

As admirable as this liberal tradition was, it turned out that economic change stimulated racial change rather than the other way around. The Southern economy was industrialized and urbanized by the forces set loose by the mobilization for World War II. A prosperous South in the 1950s was thus more open to the black liberation movement, which in turn stimulated the intervention of the federal government.

One of the most interesting questions about Southern history is why neither the liberal reform movement nor New South capitalism from within the region was ever effective enough to bring about fundamental change from within the region. Change came from the outside—the very thing that the Southern white identity group always feared and always expected. Why that was so involves a long and complex discussion, which is not appropriate here, but it has to do with the white South practicing identity politics, and especially local elites using race-baiting to protect their short-term interests. It also features the presence of abundant rewards for racial scapegoating, along with the absence of wholesome alternatives to lives of limited economic opportunity.

The lesson here is that if we want a politics free of racial and ethnic identity groups, we must do two things. We must produce a society in which such group identities are irrelevant for anything being contested through politics. That means a society that provides equal opportunity in the fullest sense to all its members, a society that protects the full citizenship rights and civil liberties of everyone. This must continue to be the goal of Southern liberals and the passionate commitment of everyone who loves freedom and believes in democracy.

We also need an American identity capacious enough to include all Americans, an identity that contains a large sphere in which we all meet as equals and as individuals with the same rights and responsibilities, bound together by a common allegiance to the core values of our revitalized democracy, and by its common though perhaps contested history. At the same time, this common arena must welcome our diverse identities of descent as being legitimately American, and allow them to persist, to borrow from and lend to each other, without imposing disadvantages on any of their members.

The answer to the question of why the Southern white identity is "unmeltable" is that it has been periodically reactivated, awakened from its wary nap by changes that are perceived as threatening by whites who themselves feel alienated, marginal, and at risk. Progressive politics thus must propose public policies and community-building initiatives that benefit working Americans of whatever racial or ethnic group, that help people acquire the capacity to help themselves, that tie individuals into the wider society and let them feel at home in the global economy. For far too long has the South followed the catastrophic economic strategy of low taxes, low public investment, low wages, and low value-added enterprises. We must test every public policy by its ability to contribute to a wholesome long-term future in an interdependent world. Above all, we must oppose the politics of division, and support the politics of inclusion.

We should be able to be both Southern AND American, just as black and white Southerners should see in each other an "other" who completes a whole. Blacks and whites in the South have been shaping each other's identity for almost four hundred years. It is impossible to think of either member of this pair without the other, and they each exist in tension with the national identity.

Our national identity has ample room for both, but meanwhile distressingly significant numbers of Southern whites will continue to spend their energies in keeping other people down until their identities become more complex, more entangled with the kudzu of the heterogeneous world, more implicated in the American identity's embrace of the universal values in what Gunnar Myrdal called the "American Creed." ■

The Southernization of American Politics

John Egerton

IN 1930, A YEAR of punishing deprivation for all Americans and especially for Southerners, a comfortably isolated clique of poets and polemicists with varying degrees of attachment to Vanderbilt University in Nashville published a book of essays titled *I'll Take My Stand* (a line borrowed from "Dixie," the chauvinistic anthem of the late Confederacy). Calling themselves the Agrarians (though they knew little or nothing about farming), the twelve writers lashed out in anger at every attempt they could uncover, however feeble, to modernize the feudal South. "Go away and leave us alone," they seemed to be saying. "We're trying to get back what we've lost, not chasing after something new."

Their timing could not have been more disconnected from reality; the stock market had crashed the previous October, sending the mother of all economic disasters, the Great Depression, on its withering, decade-long sweep across the country. The South was self-evidently desperate for modernization. The last thing it needed was a nostalgic lament for the presumed virtues of the old plantation aristocracy, recast in mythic proportion by a gentrified coterie of chauvinistic dilettantes and professorial romantics.

It is sobering now, nearly seventy-five years after the Agrarians issued their wayward screed, to find myself included in a contemporary band of dissenters who are in high dudgeon over what we see as the manifold iniquities of the South and the American nation here in the first decade of the twenty-first century. Though we approach as a motley assortment of critics from the democratic left rather than the Agrarian right, we are nonetheless out of step with the current political leadership of the United States, with the general run of elected public servants in many of our home states, and perhaps with the beliefs and convictions of the majority of rank-and-file citizens as well. Like the Agrarians, we see ourselves as a beleaguered minority, and like them, we dare to speak our minds, come what may. All similarities end there, but that is enough: We dissent. This is, thank God, still a free country.

To rise as "liberals" or "progressives" or even "moderates" and say where we stand on politics and public policy matters in this day and age is to be consciously and deliberately at cross purposes with the president of the United States, a putative Southerner; with the right-wing radicals who dominate his party, the Republicans; and with the declared values and claimed virtues of many conservative Democrats. And, to take it a step further, none of the contributors to this volume can presume to speak for the other writers in whatever remarks and assertions we make here, for there is no guarantee that we will find even ourselves in consensus over the causes or remedies or consequences of regional and national distress.

So each of us is of necessity reduced to a simple declaration: ~~This is where I stand~~ as one Southerner, one American, one voice in

JOHN EGERTON has been analyzing the themes of this essay since his 1974 book, *The Americanization of Dixie: The Southernization of America*. He has written extensively in books and articles since then about education, race, history, food, and other manifestations of Southern culture, winning the Lillian Smith Award in 1984 for *Generations: An American Family*. His other books include *Speak Now Against the Day: The Generation Before the Civil Rights Movement in the South*; *Southern Food*; and *Shades of Gray*. He lives in Nashville.

opposition to the materialistic, militaristic, ideologically driven nation we seem hell-bent upon becoming. All others, in or out of this ad hoc conjunction of alarmed essayists, will have to speak for themselves, whether they be left-wing progressives who look back in longing to the New Deal or right-wing neo-Agrarians who worship at the altar of George Bush's "new testament" imperialism.

How America got to its present disunited state of regional and national life is a cautionary tale of dark secrets, political deception, addictive greed, and lust for power that rivals the best of Shakespearean tragedy. Here is how the modern drama is playing in my head.

THERE IS A SENSE in which American politics has always had a pronounced Southern accent. Four of the first five presidents of the United States were from Virginia (though the South as a self-conscious geopolitical entity had not emerged then), and nine of the first twelve were born below the Mason and Dixon Line. In the gathering storm that boiled over into the Civil War, Southerners were influential in national affairs out of all proportion to their number, playing leading roles on both sides in the historic debate over secession. Some of them won respect for their wartime service (military as well as political), but it was the Republican commander-in-chief, Abraham Lincoln—himself of Southern stock—who articulated the determination to preserve the Union at all costs. And, by no mere coincidence, it was also this Kentucky-born president who, with the stroke of a pen, abolished slavery in the rebellious states.

In victory, Lincoln and the Union Army had put down the only insurrection ever mounted (before or since) against the "one nation, indivisible," and in time, the rebel states were gradually readmitted to the national family. But the white leadership of the South, far from conceding legal rights and political equality to even the most accomplished of African-Americans, let alone to the four million newly freed slaves, fought for a dozen years to undermine Reconstruction, the daring but poorly planned experiment in democratic nation-building. (Any resemblance to modern occupations and flawed governmental makeovers is purely accidental.)

Finally, in 1877, the federal government abandoned Reconstruction in the South, and when its agents looked away from Dixie, the region's white elected public officials and power brokers set about unhindered to resuscitate and glorify the Lost Cause of rebellion. They couldn't restore slavery, of course, but no matter; the unreconstructed rebels were more interested in gilding the lily-white myth. In their version of it, secession was not about slavery but states' rights—another noble and heroic quest for freedom, in the spirit of the colonial vanguard and the nation's Founding Fathers—and it was ruthlessly choked off by evil men who feared and hated the very idea of state sovereignty.

The so-called Compromise of 1877 was a Faustian bargain for the white South. In effect, it allowed the former Confederate states to resume their dominion over the black masses without further interference from Washington. But even as it yielded control, the Union and its component interests shrewdly reckoned that they could sustain their economic advantage over the South for as long as the defeated region chose to value white supremacy more than economic parity.

With the benefit of hindsight, the South's fateful choice helps to explain why, some sixty years later, the region still bore a stark resemblance to impoverished colonial dependencies around the globe. When other sections of the country were beginning to pull out of the Depression, the South was still paying a premium to sustain the myth of "separate but equal" segregation. Not even World War II and the peace dividend that followed would be enough to bring the region close to par with "the North" (a common shorthand tag for everyplace else). Only when court rulings, black protests, and new federal laws directly challenged segregation and white privilege would the South finally bestir itself to a grudging feint toward economic and social change.

There is a peculiar paradox embedded in this brief sketch of the post-Civil War South. Even as the region was spiraling deeper into economic chaos in the 1930s, its elected members of Congress were steadily being restored to prominence and dominance in the House and Senate. Between Vice President Andrew Johnson of Tennessee in 1865 and Vice President Lyndon Johnson of Texas in 1963, a century passed without a single Southerner taking up residence in the White House (unless you count Virginia-born Woodrow Wilson, who had had an academic career in the Northeast and was governor of New Jersey when he won the presidency for the Democrats in 1912). But when it came to senators and representatives, the South's delegations, all Democratic to the core, quickly moved from their secessionist exile to seats of authority. Because they ran unopposed for reelection almost as a matter of course, these Southerners quickly accumulated seniority and skillfully converted it into power. Even when Republicans controlled the White House, their effective majority in Congress often turned on how much cooperation and support they could attract from the tight circle of reactionary Southern Democrats.

Throughout this time of adjustment after the Civil War—indeed, from the beginning of colonial America to the modern civil rights era, a period of three and a half centuries—it seems fair to say that the single most revealing and defining feature of the South's political and cultural identity was its preoccupation with race and color. First ethnic cleansing of native tribes, then slavery, and finally legalized segregation ensured the primacy of self-described "white people" over the ones they called "red people" and "black people." Had there been no genocide and no slavery, there might well have been no rebellious South, no Civil War—and no impulse among European emigrés to abandon the liberal thirst for freedom that had emboldened them to flee religious, political, and economic tyranny in the first place.

But all of that is water over the dam now, albeit a permanent reminder of some ignominious historical realities in what we like to think of as the "sweet land of liberty." Here in the early light of the twenty-first century, there is no way we can clean the slate of history and rewrite it in terms more compatible with our stated constitutional ideals—liberty, justice, equality, and all the other ringing phrases we memorize as children. We can never hope to attain the ideals without honestly confronting and accepting responsibility for the realities. History and aspiration are inseparable. If you want to understand why the politics of the United States is looking more and more like the politics of the Old South in these ideologically charged times, you have to keep going back along the path we have taken as a nation, turning over stones along the way.

ONE LASTING LEGACY of the Civil War was the realignment of the South's voting population into a rigid new profile during the Reconstruction years. The only Southerners who cast ballots before the war were white males. Some of the time, at least, they had two or more parties to choose from; for example, four competitive candidates were on the ballot in 1860, allowing Lincoln to be elected with only 40 percent of the popular vote. But after the war, as more and more free blacks began to vote and run for office, virtually all Southern white males coalesced around the Democrats, the party of the vanquished Confederacy. Women remained excluded from the political process, and by the end of the century, black voters had dwindled to a handful—all Republicans, the party of Lincoln and the Union. Finally, the segregation laws enacted by the Southern states in the 1890s (and upheld by the

U.S. Supreme Court in 1896) disenfranchised virtually all African Americans in the region—and as a consequence, eventually ended the tenure of all black officeholders.

For the next fifty years—all the way through the presidential election of 1944—the eleven states of the old Confederacy rarely if ever broke ranks with the national Democratic party. They saw no need to; the only competition felt by incumbents came occasionally from other Democrats trying to unseat them in the primaries. It was a foregone conclusion that a small minority of white male voters (as little as 10 or 15 percent of the age-eligible electorate in some states) would send Southern incumbents back to Congress time after time, and their parliamentary skills and seniority made them indispensable, no matter which party was in the majority.

Even the liberal Franklin D. Roosevelt swept the South for the Democrats four times, from 1932 through 1944—and yet, segregation remained firmly entrenched in every state. In the election of 1948, the Magnolia Curtain parted ever so slightly when the arch-segregationist Democratic governor of South Carolina, J. Strom Thurmond, led a band of mutineers out of the party. Calling themselves the States' Rights Party (the Dixiecrats), this fringe faction won the electoral votes of Alabama, Louisiana, Mississippi, and South Carolina. (In addition, Florida gave a majority to the Republican candidate, Governor Thomas E. Dewey of New York.) But former Missouri Senator Harry S. Truman, FDR's last vice president and an open critic of segregation, still managed to pull an upset victory, thanks in large measure to Democratic majorities in the other six Southern states. Truman's margin over Dewey was 49 to 45 percent, with most of the remaining vote divided between the racist Dixiecrats and the left-wing Progressive Party led by Henry Wallace, another former vice president under Roosevelt.

The Dixiecrats soon expired as a party, and Thurmond returned without fanfare to the Democratic fold, as did most of the other

Southern politicians who had fomented rebellion with him. But their burning passion for white supremacy and segregation didn't die, and their determination to protect the racial privileges that had been written into state law and incorporated into the culture inevitably put the South on a collision course with the national Democratic Party, the U.S. Constitution, and the millions of black Southerners whose liberties had never been secured.

At the half-century mark, the Democratic Party was firmly under the thumb of Southern segregationists—not just in the states of the region but in Washington, too. Helped along by right-wing Republicans, they made Truman's life so miserable that he chose not to run again in 1952. As a former member of the exclusive club of senators and a border-state descendant of Confederates, the president had been expected to protect the "Southern way of life." Instead, he had appointed a civil rights commission and by executive order desegregated the armed services and all federal government agencies. Predictably, senior Southern Democrats responded with outrage, branding him a traitor, and both houses (again including many Republicans, whose anticommunist witch hunt somehow dovetailed with the rising anti-integrationist crusade in the South) saw to it that Truman's legislative program was torn to shreds. If he had hoped to get a little help from the region's white women, he was again doomed to disappointment; three decades after the constitutional affirmation of their right to vote, Southern females as a group showed themselves to be no more progressive than their male counterparts.

And one more blow: Even though the U.S. Supreme Court had ruled in 1944 that black citizens could no longer be locked out of party primary elections, they were still effectively excluded by poll taxes and a host of other barriers in almost all the Southern states. In the post-Civil War decades up to 1900, two black senators and twenty representatives had been elected to Congress from the South—but in the next fifty years, not a single African American from the region (and only four from the North) won a seat in either house. No one had overlooked them in the call to arms for two world wars—but even as many black men were risking their lives for democracy and freedom, the right to hold office and even to vote was systematically being stripped away from the four million-plus African Americans of voting age in the South.

AND THEN ALONG CAME *Brown*, and the Montgomery bus boycott. Looking back over the last half of the twentieth century, it is easy to spot the flashpoints of conflict over race and politics as they coursed through the Southern states like interactive surges of electric current. By the mid-1950s, a clear pattern of action and reaction was developing, highlighted by the Supreme Court's ruling against segregated schools in May 1954 and the founding of the racist White Citizens Council in Mississippi two months later; the emergent leadership of Martin Luther King, Jr., in Montgomery in 1955; the defiant Southern Manifesto issued by segregationist Southern members of Congress in 1956; and the Arkansas school desegregation crisis that erupted in Little Rock the following year.

Lawsuits attacking discrimination in employment, higher education, and the conduct of elections had been quietly wending their way through the federal courts since the mid-1930s. Black veterans of World War II showed little or no inclination to submit to discrimination, and thus faced increasing danger in confrontations with whites bent on reasserting their prewar advantage. Public places—buses, hotels, parks, restaurants, theaters—were now zones of impending friction. Change was in the wind. You could praise it or condemn it or ignore it, but eventually you were likely to be affected by it—and that prospect sparked eagerness and expectation in some, dread and anger in others.

The political reaction was especially pronounced in the Deep

South, but all of the states where segregation had been imposed by law struggled to chart their course in the approaching storm. In 1952 and again in 1956, the Republicans succeeded in sending Dwight D. Eisenhower, a popular war leader, to the White House, and Florida, Tennessee, Texas, and Virginia went along both times. But in Georgia, Mississippi, and the Carolinas, and in Alabama, where Harry Truman's name had not even been allowed on the ballot in 1948, most voters went for Democrat Adlai Stevenson twice, rather than take a chance on a Republican. In 1957, the worst fears of the most ardent Southern racists were confirmed when Eisenhower sent federal troops into Little Rock to enforce a district court's school desegregation order that Governor Orval Faubus, an opportunistic Democrat, was openly defying.

When the Democrats put up Massachusetts Senator John F. Kennedy as their presidential candidate in 1960, reactionary Southerners excoriated him as a liberal Yankee Catholic, but he still managed to carry eight states in the region; only Florida, Tennessee, and Virginia went for Kennedy's conservative GOP opponent, Richard M. Nixon.

It was then Lyndon Johnson's turn to outrage the segregationists. While he was serving out JFK's unfinished term, the persuasive Texan, a renowned master of the lawmaking process, engineered passage of the most sweeping civil rights bill in the nation's history just four months before the 1964 election. He followed that a year later with another stunning display of the fine art of political arm-twisting, the result of which was the landmark Voting Rights Act of 1965. In between those signal accomplishments, LBJ won election to a full White House term in a landslide over Republican Senator Barry Goldwater of Arizona, who carried only his home state and Alabama, Georgia, Louisiana, Mississippi, and South Carolina. On the surface, it was a crippling defeat for the Republicans—but in a full century of presidential elections since Lincoln, 1964 marked the first time the grand old party of the Union had ever defeated a Democrat in the race-obsessed, five-chambered heart of Dixie.

Leaner days were coming. South Carolina's Strom Thurmond, having used his Dixiecrat notoriety to win a write-in vote for senator in 1954, formally switched his allegiance to Goldwater and the Republican Party in 1964, signaling the start of a massive exodus from the Democratic ranks. Just as Southern blacks looking for a more promising future had transferred their loyalty from the party of Lincoln to the party of Franklin Roosevelt in a single election cycle in the 1930s, so did Southern whites begin to cross over in droves from the Democrats to the Republicans in the mid-1960s. Their motives were more complex, but in the last analysis they saw GOP conservatism as a safer haven for their racial biases than the far more liberal national Democratic Party.

The extent of this realignment was stunning. At the time of the Dixiecrat revolt in 1948, Republicans accounted for none of the South's 11 governors, none of its 22 senators and 2 of its 105 representatives in Congress, and just 3 of every 100 state legislators (50 of 1,788). But by 1974, the GOP would claim 3 of the 11 governors, 7 of 22 senators, 34 of 108 representatives, and 328 legislators (18 percent).

By Lyndon Johnson's retirement in 1968, the Republicans were beginning to fantasize about a conservative dynasty. Indeed, had it not been for the Watergate scandal, they might have enjoyed an unbroken span of two or three decades in residence at the White House. As it turned out, the GOP would still occupy 1600 Pennsylvania Avenue for twenty of the next thirty-two years. That was a remarkable feat in itself, considering the incredible string of break-ins, cover-ups, investigations, high crimes and misdemeanors that pointed to the Oval Office, and finally to President Nixon himself. Named an unindicted co-conspirator in court proceedings, he resigned office in August 1974 to avoid impeachment and trial by Congress.

It has been said that the election of Abraham Lincoln in 1860 and 1864 made every white Southerner a Democrat. In much the same way, Lyndon Johnson's influence on civil rights legislation before and after his 1964 election triumph triggered the mass exodus of white Southern Democrats to the GOP. (Johnson himself foresaw that prospect after he pushed through the Civil Rights Act of 1964, telling members of his staff, "We may have handed the South to the Republicans" for decades to come.) Across the span of a century, Lincoln and Johnson remain linked by these mirror-opposite models of cause and effect, and also by the similar fate they suffered in the prickly thicket of race and color—"The Briar Patch," as Robert Penn Warren's essay was titled in *I'll Take My Stand*.

The decade of the 1960s was an emotional bloodletting in America, a time of unrelenting conflict more intense than any since the Civil War. The black struggle for civil rights, the assassination of President Kennedy, the burgeoning peace movement and its opposition to the War in Vietnam, the spreading white resistance to all sorts of social and cultural changes, and then, in April 1968, the assassination of Martin Luther King, Jr., followed two months later by the killing of Robert Kennedy, were the most visible and momentous but by no means the only mind-altering developments of that time.

Racial injustice lay near the heart of it all. Black demands for freedom from discrimination met head-on with white resistance to virtually all manifestations of equality. And in every presidential election since 1964, that strain of pride and prejudice has remained in the bloodstream of politics—not just in the South but across the nation.

RICHARD NIXON'S COMEBACK in 1968 owed less to his own efforts than to two developments beyond his control: the anti-war campaign of liberal Senator Eugene McCarthy in the Democratic primaries, which caused President Johnson to make a late decision not to seek reelection; and the third-party candidacy of George C. Wallace, the segregationist governor of Alabama, which cut into the support of Democratic nominee Hubert Humphrey, LBJ's vice president and a longtime champion of civil rights. Wallace and Nixon carried five Southern states each, leaving only Texas to Humphrey. Also helpful to Nixon was the significant number of Gene McCarthy Democrats who stayed away from the polls.

By 1972, Nixon and his "committee to reelect the president"—CREEP—had devised a "Southern strategy" to attract the reactionary followers of Wallace and Goldwater. They succeeded as spectacularly as his gang of Watergate burglars failed. After Wallace, running again as a wild-card spoiler, was permanently crippled by an assassin's bullet on the campaign trail in May, Nixon deftly corralled the governor's base—and Wallace himself—leaving South Dakota Senator George McGovern, the Democratic nominee, with a pile of debts and a party in tatters. What Strom Thurmond started in 1948 with the Dixiecrats and reinforced in 1964 with his conversion to Republicanism was crowned in 1972 with Nixon's clean sweep of all eleven ex-Confederate states—and he did it without even bothering to campaign in the region.

The metamorphosis of Thurmond into Wallace into Nixon, the conversion of right-wing Democrats into right-wing Republicans, the translation of crude racial demagoguery into smooth code language and malevolent acts into benign promises had been accomplished in less time than anyone could have imagined. Watergate had been the only miscalculation, the only screw-up. There was Nixon, firmly in control of what appeared to be a total coup—and then, in a period of just twenty-one months, he went from having it all to losing it all, from total conquest to utter disgrace, from his election-night celebration in November 1972 to his last farewell from the steps of the White House helicopter in August 1974.

Gerald Ford, his vice president, took over and finished out the term honorably. Ford also ran a respectable campaign in 1976 against the former Democratic governor of Georgia, Jimmy Carter, a man of honesty, faith, and impeccable character—in short, an antidote to Nixon fever. But the blow to the Republicans would prove to be temporary. Carter's margin over Ford was only 51 to 49 percent, and he would not be reelected.

Two years of Ford and four of Carter had an ameliorating effect on racial politics in the South. Jimmy Carter was the first Deep South Democrat ever to win his party's nomination, and his message of reconciliation played well both North and South. When he was formally declared the nominee at the Democratic Convention in New York that July, the entire spectrum of party luminaries gathered round—his running mate Walter Mondale, the widow and father of Martin Luther King, Jr., Ted Kennedy, Jesse Jackson, Hubert Humphrey, even the wheelchair-bound George Wallace. As the strains of "We Shall Overcome" echoed through the convention hall, television cameras played over the faces of the famous and those of the thousands in attendance. Tears flowed, and millions of viewers across America, looking on in wonder, could have been excused for imagining that the South had returned at last to the circle of union, and an era of peace and progress was at hand.

The South appeared to have bought into that dream in a big way, judging by how strongly it supported the Georgia peanut farmer-politician at the polls five months later. Except for Virginia, which Ford captured by a hairbreadth, Carter swept every Southern state into the victory column of the Democratic Party—most emphatically his native Georgia, which he took by a two-to-one margin. He also won five of the six states bordering the South, where segregation laws had been in force until the mid-century or later. In the seventeen states combined, Carter's margin of victory was more than two million votes. And all this, just four years after Richard Nixon had swept through the South more convincingly than General Sherman had burned his way to the sea.

THAT DIDN'T MEAN, of course, that a moderate to liberal Southern Democrat could rescue the region permanently from the Republicans. As the nation moved away from a crisis footing on race relations and the anti-war movement at home, troubles overseas crowded to the forefront. Replacing Vietnam as the focus of American concerns were such issues as another Arab-Israeli war, chronic oil and gas shortages caused by unrest in the Middle East, surges in unemployment and inflation, a dispute over the Panama Canal, and, most devastatingly, the taking of ninety hostages at the American embassy in Iran. Through 444 agonizing days of negotiations and maneuvering, including a daring rescue attempt that failed, the American government was unable to free the captives.

In the midst of that crisis, President Carter ran for reelection against the darling of the Republican Party's radical right wing, Ronald Reagan, the movie star turned governor of California. Reagan won big—he got eight million more popular votes and ten times as many electoral votes as Carter. For the third straight time in presidential elections, the South had flip-flopped—first the Nixon-GOP sweep in 1972, then Carter's near-sweep in 1976, and now back to the Republicans in 1980, with Reagan taking everything in the region except Carter's Georgia home base.

During Reagan's eight-year reign, he owned the South (and practically everything else: against Walter Mondale in 1984, he captured forty-nine states). By the time his vice president, George H. W. Bush, had rolled over Democratic nominee Michael Dukakis in 1988—holding on to all eleven Southern states in the process—Reagan was basking in glory as the amiable titular head of a Republican dynasty. From all appearances, it was firmly in place from coast to coast—and the South was the key to the kingdom. After Bush got us into and out of a war against Iraq in the first two months of 1991, his popularity was soaring, and he seemed a sure bet for reelection.

At that point, the GOP could lay claim to having successfully grafted the limb of arch-conservative Southern Democrats onto the trunk of the national Republican Party. There had been fumbling attempts under Eisenhower, daring and partially effective ventures under Nixon, but it was Reagan who finally accomplished the feat—twice—and Bush the First then duplicated it.

Strom Thurmond, the wizened Republican senator from South Carolina, was living proof of the viability of such genetic cloning in the body politic. In his nineties, he now saw the completion of what he and the Dixiecrats had been aiming for when they fought so hard to keep their all-white party segregated in the years of sound and fury after World War II. With little more than a minor racial touch-up—the addition of a few eager African Americans, Hispanics, Asians, and East Indians of means scattered here and there—the neoconservatives of the early 1990s were road-testing a contemporary working model of *Republicanus Invincibilis*, the Unbeatable Republican.

Their big picture, their grand dream, was of a party of privilege, an elite establishment controlled by men and women of wealth and station who loved power and would do whatever it took to get it and use it. Tax-and-spend liberals would be rendered extinct; unfettered free enterprise in a market economy would be the only way to go. Some government regulation and oversight might be needed from time to time if it promised to further the cause of selective privilege, but it would have to be financed with borrowed money or through privatization, rather than with new taxes. Civil liberties would be subject to review by the ruling authorities. The three branches of government would not be coequal but rank-ordered, with the executive on top and the judiciary on the bottom. The primary role of government would be to fight wars, aid in natural disasters, uphold their version of Judeo-Christian values, and secure the nation's ruling class and their assets against terrorist threats.

In essence, this ideology was Darwinian but not evolutionary; it served notice on all who cared to listen that a revolution was coming, and only the fittest would survive. There would be expectations but no required litmus test with respect to specific positions on hot-button social issues such as gun control, abortion, capital punishment, school prayer, homosexuality, immigration, even race; you could quietly identify with a more liberal view on a few of those, as long as you didn't make a scene. (Such silent free choice might not extend, however, to your views on affirmative action, the Patriot Act, or preemptive war.) If you aspired to be or already were rich and privileged, and loyally supported the Republican regime with your time and money, and obeyed the golden rule of capitalism (those who have the gold make the rules), you had a prepaid ticket to the revolution, and a box seat for the feature event: the feeding of the donkeys to the Christians.

Democrats were not exactly lining up for this banquet. Not many wanted to take a shot at the seemingly unbeatable George Bush in 1992, but there were a few—and the luckiest among them turned out to be Bill Clinton, the former governor of Arkansas. As the last candidate left standing after a grueling primary season, he found himself running against an incumbent president whose fortunes were being sucked into the downdraft of an economic tailspin after the Gulf War.

In the hope of passing himself off as a Texan and a Southerner,

Bush kept a hotel address and his voter registration in Houston, but that golden parachute would not be strong enough to save him. Ross Perot, a genuine Texas maverick with money to burn, ended up in the herd with Bush and Clinton, and when the dust settled, it was Perot's huge third-party total—nineteen million votes—that made the difference in Clinton's upset victory, by 43 to 38 percent, over President Bush, a bonafide Connecticut Yankee who, Texas Governor Ann Richards memorably said, "was born with a silver foot in his mouth."

The eight-year tenure of Bill Clinton in the White House was almost too eventful to be summarized here. Let it suffice to say that he was a Southerner, a centrist in the Democratic Party, a master politician, a policy wonk, a genuine reconciler on racial and social issues, and a good-time guy with a roving eye. Not only did he unseat an incumbent; he also won reelection in 1996, beating the longtime Senate Republican leader, Bob Dole of Kansas, by a comfortable margin. Both times, incidentally, Clinton received less than a majority of the popular vote, and both times he carried only four Southern states, but he prevailed nonetheless.

The better he was at everything he did, good and bad, the more he was demonized by the Republican establishment. (Jimmy Carter, who was Sunday-School pure in contrast to Clinton, was also scathingly denounced by the sacrosanct Republicans.) When Clinton's escapades—his "zipper problem," as some called it—spilled out into public view, there followed a sensational culture war that left no parties uninjured. After months of charges and countercharges, investigations, depositions, leaks, sensational testimony, and bills of impeachment accusing him of lying under oath and other crimes, Bill Clinton was tried and acquitted by the one hundred members of the U.S. Senate. The Republicans had made the fatal mistake of trying to hang a morals rap on the president of the United States—and in Washington, D.C., of all places, where the pure in heart are an endangered species. After a few self-righteous Republican accusers were made to suffer from their own indecent exposure, others grew more circumspect. At the end of his second term, Clinton walked away shaken but under his own power, leaving to history the final evaluation of his tenure. On that point, the American people seemed to be divided down the middle. Most Democrats, and even a good many Republicans, acknowledged his great intellectual and political skills—but practically all, from blind adherents to enraged haters, were dumbstruck at the magnitude of what he risked and what he lost to slake his sexual thirst.

And so the stage was set for the election of 2000—the longest and closest presidential slugfest in American history, and by any measure one of the most controversial and divisive.

FOR A VARIETY OF REASONS having to do with geography, history, political ideology, and race (not to mention an evanescent quality implied by the title of a 1977 book by David Leon Chandler: *The Natural Superiority of Southern Politicians*), the South, by whatever definition, is now hugely important, if not indispensable, to a successful run for the White House. Conspicuous by its imposing presence in the formative decades of the nation, and by its near-total absence for a century after the Civil War, the region has become the eight hundred-pound, stogie-puffing gorilla in the smoke-filled rooms of national politics since the movement for civil rights was at high tide forty years ago.

In the nineteen presidential elections prior to the Civil War, fully half of the winning and losing candidates (including major third-party contenders) had Southern roots. But in the twenty-five elections that followed, through 1960, only borderline Southerners made the list, and they were few in number—Lincoln, Wilson, and Truman among the winners, John W. Davis and the ubiquitous

Strom Thurmond the only losers.

In the last ten national campaigns, from 1964 through 2000, the South has made a dramatic return to the presidential battlefield, providing fully half the finalists. Lyndon Johnson, Jimmy Carter, and Bill Clinton won four times among them, and Carter lost once, as did George Wallace and Ross Perot. (George Bush the First also belongs on the list, as a winner and a loser, if his Houston postal address is considered valid.) And in the election of 2000, Al Gore and George Bush the Second got top billing in the Democratic and Republican columns on the ballot, marking the first time two Southerners had vied for the presidency. Both gave off more of an Ivy League aura than convincing Southern verisimilitude, but they unabashedly claimed bloodlines to the one region above all others where a strong showing was absolutely essential to national victory. The Southernization of American politics had finally come to pass.

There is no point in replaying the championship bout between Gore and Bush—the bruising campaign, the Clinton factor, the incredibly high stakes, the election-night drama, the five weeks of sudden-death overtime, Gore's 540,000-vote margin of victory at the polls, Bush's 271-269 margin in electoral votes, Gore's crushing loss in his home state of Tennessee, and Bush's margin of a few hundred votes in the decisive state of Florida, where a recount was halted by a five-to-four decision of the U.S. Supreme Court. Millions of words have already been written on the election, and there will be millions more—but it's impossible to imagine that the hard feelings on either side will ever fade away. The drama was so intense, the debate so divisive, the nation so polarized that even now the angry rhetoric still echoes like a distant rumble of thunder.

That election has been over for three years; nothing will ever change the outcome. What is at issue now is how President Bush has conducted himself in office, and whether he will be reelected. My acknowledged liberal bias will leave no doubt about the convictions I hold on these matters. To my mind, he is the worst president in memory (and I remember back to Roosevelt). Compared to Bush, Ronald Reagan and Richard Nixon were brilliant thinkers and great statesmen. In three years, he has turned a half-trillion-dollar surplus into a half-trillion-dollar deficit. Bankruptcies, loan foreclosures, devalued currency, recession—all signs of economic distress—have mushroomed on his watch, and almost three million jobs have vanished from our economy. Congress is as bitterly polarized now as when Bill Clinton was caught up in the Monica Lewinsky scandal. Shameless pandering to special interest groups, from the religious right to corporate big spenders, has been a Bush hallmark, as has criminal behavior by corporate executives with close ties to the President and to Vice President Dick Cheney.

After renegade terrorists from the Middle East killed more than three thousand persons in coordinated sneak attacks in the United States on September 11, 2001, President Bush retaliated by pursuing known perpetrators into Afghanistan and, in March of 2003, launching an unrelated preemptive invasion of Iraq under false pretenses. At this writing, a thousand American and allied soldiers had already died in the two countries; no one will say how many military and civilian deaths there have been on the other side, but informed estimates are between 20,000 and 100,000. In another part of the Middle East, Arabs and Israelis no longer think the U.S. can help end their violent deadlock. The diplomatic reputation of our country is at its lowest ebb in decades—and this just twenty-eight months past 9/11, when a worldwide outpouring of sympathy washed over us.

There is much more in the indictment, but let it pass for now; this is enough to alarm many more conservative than I, from United Nations officials and "Old Europe" leaders to some Bush administration diplomats, cabinet members, military brass, Republicans in Congress—and even his father, the former president, whose own memoir spells out detailed arguments against the occupation of Iraq that his son discarded one by one in his zeal to overthrow its dictator, Saddam Hussein.

But none of this will be directly instrumental in the reelection or ousting of George W. Bush in November 2004. His fate will be decided by one hundred million voters who love him or hate him (there is no middle ground), who weigh his assets and liabilities against those of his Democratic opponent, and who will also be making a value judgment on the relative merits of the two political parties.

It is this last point that is most troubling, for the harsh fact is that neither Democrats nor Republicans are in good standing with the American electorate. To be sure, there are significant ideological differences between the two parties, but they are equally flawed institutions in many respects, and both deserve much of the criticism leveled by citizens who have simply lost their faith and trust in politicians, parties, and the democratic process. These are a few of the many reasons for this disillusionment:

Both parties give lip service to campaign finance reform and other election changes, but neither is serious enough to apply failsafe standards to the process. (Any country that can find multiple ways to make lotteries and automatic teller machines trustworthy and efficient can figure out how to receive, count, and report the votes of its citizens.) Similarly, why should we believe that neither party can fix what's broke in the Social Security system, or government-approved retirement programs, or Medicare/Medicaid—when we observe both parties working together to make sure their own pay and perks never suffer from neglect?

Democrats and Republicans alike voted in favor of Bush's war in Iraq. Both have performed ineptly—or worse—in the conduct of the so-called "war on drugs." Neither has an equitable immigration policy. Neither has ever found ways to overhaul and simplify the federal income tax code. Both serve themselves generously from the federal pork barrel, where all freebies great and small originate. Each party blocks judicial appointments of the other, while piously blaming "those obstructionists" across the aisle. Neither has provided effective leadership in seeking viable compromise on such issues as abortion, capital punishment, gun control, gay rights, universal health care, price controls on prescription drugs, diplomatic relations with Cuba, or environmental protection.

Systemic dysfunction of this magnitude not only alienates half or more of the citizenry; it allows misfeasance and malfeasance to spread undetected through the entire structure of government, from the White House to the courthouse. In the present instance, it has led to the installation of George W. Bush, a self-described cowboy and a Southerner, in the White House—the first Republican from this region ever to hold the office of president—and his administration is running the federal government as you might imagine the Confederates having done if they had won the Civil War. It is almost as if we had come full circle, back to a time of blatant discrimination and arrogant disdain for human rights—not driven directly by race and ethnicity this time, but by economic and ideological favoritism disguised in the wardrobe of family values, Judeo-Christian piety, compassionate conservatism, deregulation of free enterprise, privatization of government services, corporate welfare, globalization of trade, extreme patriotism in the war on terror, and imperialism in the name of "preemptive defense."

No longer are we presented with the once-shocking spectacle of Southern Democrats crossdressing as national Republicans. As the new millennium marches on, the audience on both sides of the aisle has grown weary of the charade. The thrill is gone. The South is owning up at last to the fact that all those right-wing Democratic poseurs truly are Republicans. With the plotting and scheming finally at an end, the neo-cons have dropped their capes and stepped out in all their nakedness, showing themselves as they now want to be seen, come what may. The pretenders had crossed over for good—from the same old party to the Grand Old Party.

As painful as this divorce may be for some, there's no doubt that it's for the best. Since *Brown* changed the political landscape a half-century ago, the Democrats have been holding back, trying to persuade their right-wing cabal of old-guard, mostly Southern segregationists not to go storming out in anger, as their Dixiecrat and Rebel forebears had done.

The party abandoned its New Deal legacy as a positive force for change and hunkered down behind a defensive shield. The leaders failed to comprehend that Harry Truman and Lyndon Johnson died for their sins, and in so doing freed the Democrats to reclaim their heritage as the fountainhead of egalitarian opportunity.

But instead of accepting the challenge, the party has spent most of the past forty years wandering in the political wilderness, too timid to take up the fight, while Richard Nixon and Ronald Reagan and the Bushes were following a Southern strategy of "colorblind" patriotism and materialism that cloaked the Republican tilt toward an overwhelmingly white and privileged elite. Notwithstanding the solid accomplishments of the Carter and Clinton administrations—or, for that matter, their shortcomings—it is the Democratic Party, from the national headquarters down to the precinct level, that has lost the courage and confidence to say for whom and for what it stands.

Meanwhile, forty years after LBJ pushed through the Civil Rights Act of 1964, the Southern Republicans have gone from no governors to 7 of 11; from no senators to 13 of 22; from 7 House members to 76 of 131; and from 60 state legislators to 846 of 1,782. And all of these governors and members of Congress are white, as are all but a small fraction of the legislators.

And where are the African Americans? On the Democratic side. Half of the 600 or so black legislators in the nation are serving in the 11 Southern states; 16 of the 38 members of the Congressional Black Caucus, all Democrats, represent these same states; and almost two-thirds of the 9,000-plus black elected officials in the country—Democrats, overwhelmingly—are in the South.

Sixty years ago, as World War II was ending, there were no black officeholders in the South—and probably fewer than 200 in the entire U.S., including just two in Congress and 28 in state legislatures. Fewer than 5 percent of African American adults in the South were registered to vote. Today, the percentage of black voters is roughly equal to that of whites, and the Democratic Party has been their pathway to political participation.

What's more, the Democratic presidents with Southern roots over the past half-century—Truman, Johnson, Carter, Clinton—each did more to expand the basic rights and opportunities of black citizens than all the other presidents, Democrat and Republican, since Lincoln.

Instead of trying to placate their foot-dragging right-wing reactionaries, who since the time of FDR have been Democrats in name only, it is time, past time, for Democrats to forget them. Bona fide Democrats need to be reaching out to their natural constituency—young people, the working class, women, African Americans, immigrants, the elderly, the poor, small business owners, and all the millions of middle-class citizens who have been whipsawed by the greedy elite, losing their jobs, their health insurance, their retirement funds, their schools and colleges, their homes. Now, all that stands between these loyal, hard-working Americans and a permanent condition of underclass subjugation is the Democratic Party.

In November, George W. Bush must stand for reelection against the chosen Democratic challenger, Senator John Kerry of

Massachusetts. Once again, Bush will benefit from the presence of a familiar third name on the presidential ballot—that of the quixotic Ralph Nader. Until the recent eruption of new violence and disorder in Iraq, the Bush regime was confidently and gleefully anticipating a global reign of empire in "the New Republican Century." They still take smug comfort in their certitude that the hand of destiny is guiding this crusade, just as it delivered the solid South to them four years ago.

Only two slender reeds of hope still beckon to the uncounted millions of alarmed but disorganized Bush opponents, whether they live in the South or elsewhere.

One is the greed factor: The Republicans want it all and want it now, and in their haste to grab it, they might overreach—as Nixon did in the early 1970s, as Bush the First did in the early 1990s, and as his son the sitting president is prone to do now. That could happen.

And second, there is always a chance that a critical mass of progressive Southerners and their democratic allies elsewhere will wise up to the all-hat, no-cattle dude rancher who got us into this mess, and mount an all-out effort to drive his measley herd out to pasture.

All across the country, a new majority of Americans hungry for reform is milling about, hoping to bump into a leader. A multitude of concerns pulls them this way and that—but if there is a single deep belief they all hold in common, it is this: The reelection of George W. Bush on November 2, 2004, and the further entrenchment of the political ideology he represents, will be the undoing of America.

Beating "those people" (to use Robert E. Lee's phrase) will be a tremendous challenge. Thanks to their rich patrons, the Republicans will have a quarter-billion-dollar war chest to finance their "shock and awe" offensive, and they have numerous weapons of mass deception in their arsenal. They aim to keep virtually all the states Bush took before—including the South's eleven—and add several more. Another solid South probably would clinch a second Bush term; the other thirty-nine states can't be expected to overcome a handicap that large. There can be no peaceable regime change in Washington without a strong assist from progressive Southerners. Can we lay aside our differences and pull together? Perhaps—but our track record for such cooperative behavior is not very impressive, and we've seldom shown a knack for spotting the rainmakers and false prophets in our midst.

Still, a frail hope is better than no hope at all. It ain't over 'til it's over. ■

Notes

To "Standing on the Promises," pages 45–60.
[1] Quotations from Thomas Merton are from his 1966 essay, "Blessed Are the Meek: The Christian Roots of Non-Violence," included in Thomas Merton, *Passion for Peace: The Social Essays*, ed. William H. Shannon (New York: Crossroad, 1995) p. 252]
[2] The reference to Colin Powell and Norman Schwarzkopf is from Harry G. Summers, Jr., *A Critical Analysis of the Gulf War* (New York, 1992), p. 54.

To "Ignoring Inequality," pages 61–69.
[1] See *Leandro v. State*, 488 S.E.2d 249 (N.C. Sup.Ct. 1997).
[2] Rorty, Richard, *Achieving Our Country: Leftist Thought in Twenty-First Century America*, 86-89 (1998).
[3] Jeff Madrick, "Inequality and Democracy," *The Fight is for Democracy*, p. 26 (George Packer, ed. Perennial Books, 2003).
[4] Quoted in Roger Cramton, "Mandatory Pro Bono," 19 *Hofstra L.Rev.* 1113, 1118-9 (1991).
[5] See generally, Deborah Rhode, "Access to Justice," 69 *Fordham L. Rev.* 1785 (2001); and Deborah H. Rhode, *In the Interests of Justice: Reforming the Legal Profession* (2000).
[6] Kennedy, David M., *Freedom from Fear: The American People in Depression and War, 1929-1945* at 280 (1999).
[7] Bailyn, Bernard, *Faces of Revolution: Personalities and Themes in the Struggle for American Independence* 220 (1990).

To "My Yellow Ribbon Town," pages 70–86.
[1] Thomas Powers, "The Vanishing Case for War," *The New York Review of Books*, December 4, 2003, pp. 14, 15.
[2] Arundhati Roy, "Instant-Mix Imperial Democracy," a speech at the Riverside Church, New York, May 13, 2003.
[3] Paul M. Gaston, *The New South Creed: A Study in Southern Mythmaking*, published originally by Knopf in 1970; the second edition, with a new afterword by me, was published by NewSouth Books in 2002.
[4] Ernest B. Gaston, "True Cooperative Individualism: An Argument on the Plan of the Fairhope Industrial Association," *Liberty Bell*, April 28, 1894. See also, Paul M. Gaston, *Man and Mission: E. B. Gaston and the Origins of the Fairhope Single Tax Colony* (Montgomery: Black Belt Press, 1993).
[5] Quoted in Gaston, *Man and Mission*, p. 140.
[6] *Ibid.*, esp. pp. 4, 139-140.
[7] Fairhope *Courier*, January 1, 1895.
[8] John Dewey visited the school in 1913 and wrote glowingly about it. "The democracy which proclaims equality of opportunity as its ideal requires an

education in which learning and social application, ideas and practice, work and recognition of the meaning of what is done, are united from the beginning and for all," he wrote. The Fairhope school, he believed, clearly showed "how the ideal of equal opportunity for all is to be transmuted into reality." John and Evelyn Dewey, *Schools of Tomorrow* (New York, 1915), pp. 315-16. See also my biography of Marietta Johnson, founder and longtime director of the school, in Paul M. Gaston, *Women of Fair Hope* (Athens: University of Georgia Press, 1984), ch. 3.
9 The quotations and some of the language here may be found in a speech I gave in 1997, later published in pamphlet form: Paul M. Gaston, *My South—and Yours* (Charlottesville, 1997), pp. 5-6.
10 David and Holly Franke, *Safe Places East* (New York, 1973), pp. 42-69.
11 Fairhope *Courier,* April 1, 1898.
12 Quoted in Larry Allums, *Fairhope, 1894-1994: A Pictorial History* (Virginia Beach, 1994), p. 156.
13 *Ibid.,* p. 179.

To "Our Imperiled Union," pages 87–102.
1 *Washington Post,* 4/13/03.
2 Bk. 5, ch II, Part 2.
3 *Common Sense,* page 40 ff, Signet Classic ed.
4 *The Washington Spectator,* 8/1/03.
5 *Washington Post,* 7/14/03.
6 Washington Post, 5/30/03.
7 *Washington Post.*
8 *Washington Post,* 9/25/03.
9 *Reflections on the Revolution in France.* Penguin Classics, pages 194-5.

To "Civil Liberties in a Time of Crises," pages 121–146.
1 Thomas Jefferson, Notes on the State of Virginia. (1781-1785) Query XVIII.
2 February 12, 2003. It takes courage to speak out against them. Al Gore, the Democratic standard bearer in the 2000 election, is one of the few who stands by the Constitution. He accused President Bush, his erstwhile opponent, of "exploiting public fears for partisan political gain, of using the war against terrorism for partisan advantage." He challenged the Bush assumption that we have to give up our traditional freedoms to be safe from terrorists. American citizens, Gore said, "seized on American soil should not be held without end, isolated in a Navy brig without being charged, without being tried, without counsel, without being able to contact their families. It is simply not enough to pin the label "enemy combatant" on them.
3 "Beware the leader who bangs the drums of war in order to whip the citizenry into a patriotic fervor, for patriotism is indeed a double-edged sword. It emboldens the blood, just as it narrows the mind, and when the drums of war have reached a fever pitch, the leader will have no need in seizing the rights of the citizenry. Rather, the citizenry, infused with fear and blinded by patriotism, will offer up all their rights unto the leader, and gladly so." Attributed to Julius Caesar on the network chat rooms, but not to be found

in Shakespeare.

[4] "The right of the people to be secure in their persons, houses, papers and effects, against unreasonable searches and seizures, shall not be violated, and no Warrants shall issue, but upon probable cause supported by oath or affirmation, and particularly describing the place to be searched, and the person or things to be seized."

[5] *Entick v. Carrington*, 19 Howell's State Trials 1029 (1765).

[6] The late Supreme Court Justice Robert Jackson warned that the Congress War Power is the "most dangerous to free government. It is usually invoked in haste and excitement when calm legislative consideration is difficult. It is executed in a time of patriotic fervor that makes moderation unpopular, and worst of all it is interpreted by judges under the influence of the same passions and pressures."

[7] "An Unpatriotic Act," editorial *New York Times*, August 25, 2003.

[8] *United States v. United States District Court*, 407 U.S. 297, 317 (1972).

[9] 407 U.S. at 322, 323.

[10] "Washington Bends The Rules," *New York Times*, August 22, 2002.

[11] "Court Overturns Limits On Wiretaps to Combat Terror," *New York Times*, November 19, 2002.

[12] "U.S. Uses Terror Law to Pursue Crimes From Drugs to Swindling," *New York Times*, Sept 28, 2003.

[13] "Surveillance, Search Warrants at all-time high," Raleigh, *News and Observer*, May 3, 2003.

[14] "Washington Bends the Rules," *New York Times*, August 22, 2002.

[15] "Opponents Lose Challenge to Government's Broader Use of Wiretaps to Fight Terrorism," *New York Times*, March 25, 2003.

[16] John Southerden Burn, *The Star Chamber*, London Russell Smith (1870).

[17] *Ibid.*

[18] *Stanley v. Georgia*, 394 U.S. 557 (1969).

[19] "New Tools for Domestic Spying, and Qualms," *New York Times*, Dec. 10, 2002.

[20] "Some Librarians Use Shredder to Show Opposition to New FBI Powers," *New York Times*, April 7, 2003.

[21] "Some Librarians Oppose Searches," *New York Times*, June 25, 2002.

[22] "Justice Department Lists Use of New Power to Fight Terror," May 21, 2003

[23] "Ashcroft Mocks Librarians and Other Who Oppose Parts of Counterterrorism Law," *New York Times*, September 16, 2003.

[24] Michael Curtis, *Free Speech*, *"The People's Darling Privilege," Duke University Press* (2000), pp. 289-296.

[25] Pollitt, "Equal Protection in Public Education: 1954–61," *AAUP Bulletin*, Autumn 1961, p. 197.

[26] "New Agency Will Not Lie, Top Pentagon Officials Say," *New York Times*, Feb. 21, 2002.

[27] "Managing the News," editorial, *New York Times*, Feb. 20, 2002.

[28] "Office of Strategic Mendacity," *New York Times*, Feb. 20, 2002.

[29] "Rumsfeld Says He May Drop New Office of Influence," *New York Times*, Feb. 25, 2002.

[30] "Pentagon and Bogus News: All Is Denied," *New York Times*, Decem

[31] Matthew Rothschild, "The No Fly List," *The Progressive Magazine*, June, 2002.

Notes 227

32 "Airport Security Story," *New York Times,* September 15, 2003.
33 "No-Fly data base prompts lawsuit," Raleigh, *News and Observer,* April 23, 2003.
34 Rothschild, *The No-Fly List,* Ibid.
35 The Sixth Amendment to the U.S. Constitution.
36 Martha Young, *The Salem Witch Trials,* 64 Tulane Law Review 235 (1989); Jane Moriarty, *Wonder of the Invisible World,* 26 Vermont Law Review 42 (2001).
37 William Rehnquist, *All the Laws But One,* Alfred Knopf (1998).
38 Rehnquist, note 38 *supra* at 60.
39 Curtis, note 40 *supra* at p. 301.
40 "Kangaroo Courts," *New York Times,* Nov. 26, 2001.
41 "In Letter 300 Law Professors Oppose Tribunals Plan," *New York Times,* December 8, 2001.
42 "Rights Official Criticizes U.S. Tribunal Plan," *New York Times,* Dec. 8, 2001.
43 "Tribunals Move From Theory to Reality," *New York Times,* July 4, 2003.
44 "Six Detainees Soon May Face Military Trials," *New York Times,* July 4, 2003.
45 "2 Britons, Australian Among Six Facing Trial," *Washington Post,* July 5, 2003.
46 "Families of 2 British Terrorism Suspects Oppose Military Trials by the U.S.," *New York Times,* July 5, 2003.
47 "Bowing to Ally, Bush to Rethink Tribunals for British Subjects," *New York Times,* July 19, 2003.
48 "Death Penalty Ruled Out For Two British Detainees," *New York Times,* July 23, 2003.
49 "U.S. Satisfies Australia on Possible Terror Trial," *New York Times,* July 24, 2003.
50 "Pentagon Issues Instructions For Trials Before Military Commissions," "Legal News," *U.S. Law Week,* Vol. 71, No. 45 May 27, 2003.
51 "Rules Set Up for Terror Tribunal May Better Some Defense Lawyers," *New York Times,* July 13, 2003.
52 "U.S. Erecting a Solid Prison at Guantanamo for Long Term," *New York Times,* Oct. 22, 2003.
53 "Bush Reconsidering stand on Treating Captives of War," *New York Times,* January 29, 2002 .
54 "U.S. Erecting a Solid Prison at Guantanamo for Long Term," *New York Times,* Oct. 22, 2003.
55 "Criticized, U.S. Brings Visitors to Camp," *New York Times,* January 26, 2002.
56 "Afghans Freed from Guantanamo Speak of Heat and Isolation," *New York Times,* October 29, 2002.
57 "More Prisoners to be Released from Guantanamo," *New York Times,* May 6, 2003.
58 "U.S. in Talks to Return Scores Held at Cuba Site," *New York Times,* December 1, 2003.
59 "Rumsfeld Backs Plan to Hold Captives Even if Acquitted," *New York Times,* March 29, 2003.
60 "A P.O.W. Tangle, What the Law Says," *New York Times,* January 29, 2003.
61 "Prisoners, Surely, But P.O.W.'s?," *New York Times,* January 27, 2002.
62 "Detainers are not P.O.W.'s, Cheney and Rumsfeld Declare," *New York Times,* January 21, 2002.
63 "Criticized, U.S. Brings Visitors to Prison Camp," *New York Times,* January 26, 2002

[64] "The Guantanamo Scandal," *New York Times,* May 15, 2003.
[65] "Try Detainees or Free Them, 3 Senators Urge," *New York Times,* December 13, 2003
[66] "Twelve Kuwaitis Challenge Guantanamo Detention," Raleigh, *News and Observer,* October 16, 2002.
[67] "Judge Rebuffs Detainees at Guantanamo," *New York Times,* August 1, 2002.
[68] "Bush Administration Wins Court Victory on Guantanamo Detentions," *New York Times,* March 12, 2003.
[69] "Justice To Hear Case of Detainees at Guantanamo," *New York Times,* November 11, 2003.
[70] "U.S. Courts Reject Detention Policy in 2 Terror Cases," *New York Times,* December 19, 2003.
[71] "Federal Sweep Shifts Attitude of Immigrants about the U.S.," *New York Times,* December 5, 2001.
[72] "On the Inside Looking Out, Caught in a Net of Suspicion," *New York Times,* Oct. 8, 2001.
[73] "Egyptian Student cleared in 9/11 Attack May Sue," *New York Times,* January 21, 2002.
[74] "Detainees Abuse Is Detailed," *New York Times,* December 19, 2003; "Tapes show abuse of 9/11 detainees," Raleigh, *News and Observer,* December 18, 2003.
[75] "Justice Dept. And Senate Clash Over Bush Actions," *New York Times,* November 29, 2001.
[76] "Al-Qaeda Link Seen In Only a Handful of 1,200 Detainees," *New York Times,* November 29, 2001.
[77] "Ashcroft Offers Accounting of 641 charged or Held," *New York Times,* Nov. 29, 2001.
[78] "Closed Immigration Hearings Criticized as Prejudicial," *New York Times,* December 7, 2001.
[79] The words are those of Judge Damon Keith who wrote the opinion for the Sixth Circuit. See Bob Herbert, "Sorrow and Liberties," *New York Times,* October 19, 2002.
[80] Hentoff, *The First Freedom,* pp. 113-122 (1980).
[81] "The war on dissent," *Arkansas Times,* Oct. 19, 2001; *The Cincinnati Post,* Feb. 23, 1998.
[82] "Bush Has Widened Authority of C.I.A. to Kill Terrorists," *New York Times,* December 15, 2002.
[83] "Al-Qaeda suspects aren't treated with kid glovers," Raleigh, *News and Observer,* December 27, 2002.
[84] *CCR News,* a release of the Center for Constitutional Rights, Fall, 2003
[85] "The Saga of a Leak," *New York Times,* October 5, 2003.
[86] "A Top Bush Aid Didn't Identify C.I.A. Agent, White House Says," *New York Times,* September 30, 2003.
[87] "Iraq Arms Critic Reacts to Report on Wife," *New York Times,* Aug. 8, 2003.
[88] "The Right Thing, at Last," editorial, *New York Times,* December 31, 2003.
[89] "Ashcroft Elects Not to Supervise Inquiry On Leak," *New York Times,* December 31, 2003.
[90] "Ashcroft Defends Antiterror Plan, Says Criticism May Aid U.S. Foes," *New*

York Times, December 7, 2001.
[91] *Olmstead v. United States*, 277 U.S. 438 (1928). Brandeis was speaking about government wiretapping.
[92] "Arab-Americans Are Finding New Tolerance Amid Turmoil," *New York Times*, September 22, 2002.
[93] "Arabs and Muslims Steer Through an Unsettling Scrutiny," *New York Times*, September 12, 2001.
[94] "Attacks and Harassment of Middle-Eastern Americans Rising," *New York Times*, September 14, 2001.
[95] "In Sacramento a Publisher's Questions Draw the Wrath of the Crowd," *New York Times*, December 20, 2001.
[96] "At Berkeley, a New Dispute Over Words From Long Ago," *New York Times*, January 1, 2003.
[97] "Now Berkeley Lets Words of Anarchist Stay in Letter," New York Times, January 17, 2003.
[98] "Chicks cheered at start of U.S. tour," Raleigh, *News and Observer*, May 2, 2003.
[99] "Poetry Makes Nothing Happen?," *The Nation*, February 23, 2003.

To "Democracy Cannot Be Exported," pages 169–180.

[1] Statement of C. Vann Woodward before the U.S. House of Representatives, June 24, 1981.
[2] S.Rep. No. 417, 97th Cong., 2d Sess. 10 (1982), reprinted in 1982 *U.S. Code Cong. & Adm. News* 187.
[3] Chandler Davidson & Bernard Grofman, eds., *Quiet Revolution in the South: The Impact of the Voting Rights Act 1965-1990* (Princeton, N.J.: Princeton University Press, 1994), p. 336.
[4] *Georgia v. Ashcroft*, 195 F.Supp.2d 25, 95 (D.D.C. 2002).
[5] Hearings before the Committee on the Judiciary, United States Senate, Eighty-ninth Congress, First Session, on S. 1564 to enforce the 15th Amendment to the Constitution of the United States, p. 621.
[6] LBJ Library, LE/HU 2-7, Box. 70.
[7] Hearings before the Subcommittee on Constitutional Rights of the Committee on the Judiciary, United States Senate, Ninety-first Congress, First and Second Sessions, on S. 818, S. 2456, S. 2507, and Title IV of S. 2029, Bills to Amend the Voting Rights Act of 1965, p. 351.
[8] *Id.* at 669.
[9] *Id.* at 449.
[10] H.Rep. No. 397, 91st Cong., 2d Sess. (1970), reprinted in 1970 *U.S. Code Cong. & Adm. News* 3281.
[11] *Atlanta Constitution*, October 22, 1970.
[12] David L. Norman to Arthur K. Bolton, February 11, 1972.
[13] Extension of the Voting Rights Act of 1965, Hearings before the Subcommittee on Constitutional Rights of the Committee on the Judiciary, United States Senate, Ninety-fourth Congress, First Session, on S. 407, S. 903, S. 1297, S. 1409, and S. 1443, Arthur Bolton to Sen. John Tunney.
[14] Extension of the Voting Rights Act, Hearings before the Subcommittee on Civil and Constitutional Rights of the Committee on the Judiciary, House of Representatives, Ninety-fourth Congress, First Session, on H.R. 939, H.R.

2148, H.R. 3247, and H.R. 3501, p. 63.
[15] S.Rep. No. 295, 94th Cong. 1st Sess. 17 (1975), reprinted in 1975 *U.S. Code Cong. & Adm. News*, 783.
[16] *Busbee v. Smith*, 549 F. Supp. 494, 507 (D.C.D. 1982).
[17] *Id.* at 501.
[18] Voting Rights Act, Hearings before the Subcommittee on the Constitution of the Committee on the Judiciary, United States Senate, Ninety-seventh Congress, Second Session, on S. 53, S. 1761, S. 1992, and H.R. 3112, Bills to Amend the Voting Rights Act of 1965, pp. 942, 950.
[19] Extension of the Voting Rights Act, Hearings before the Subcommittee on Civil and Constitutional Rights of the Committee on the Judiciary, House of Representatives, Ninety-seventh Congress, First Session, pp. 86, 208, 224, 590, 2068.
[20] David A. Bositis, *Redistricting and Representation: The Creation of Majority-Minority Districts and the Evolving Party System in the South* (Washington, D.C.: Joint Center for Political & Economic Studies, 1995), p. 28.
[21] David T. Canon, "Redistricting and the Congressional Black Caucus," 23 *American Political Quarterly* 159, 160-61 (1995).
[22] Frank R. Parker, "The Constitutionality of Racial Redistricting: A Critique of *Shaw v. Reno*," 3 *D.C. Law Review* 1, 19-20 (1995).
[23] Brief of Appellant State of Georgia, pp. 28, 31, 40-1.
[24] *Georgia v. Ashcroft*, 123 S. Ct. 2498, 2510-11 (2003).
[25] Brief of Appellant State of Georgia, p. 16.
[26] *Citizens for a Better Gretna v. City of Gretna, La.*, 636 F. Supp. 1113, 1121 (E.D.La. 1986).
[27] *Colleton County Council v. McConnell*, 201 F.Supp.2d 618, 643 (D.S.C. 2002).
[28] *Yick Wo v. Hopkins*, 118 U.S. 356, 370 (1886).

To "Identity Politics, Southern Style," pages 169–180.

[1] Henry Louis Gates, *New York Times*, March 27, 1994. Also see "Goodbye, Columbus? Notes on the Culture of Criticism," *American Literary History*, 3 (1991), pp. 711-727; and "The Meaning of America," *New Yorker*, April 19, 1993, pp. 113-117. Gates is the Director of the W.E.B. DuBois Center at Harvard University.
[2] Jean Bethke Elshtain, *Democracy On Trial* (New York: Basic Books, 1995), p. 66. Elshtain is the Laura Spelman Rockefeller Professor of Social and Political Ethics at the University of Chicago.
[3] Schlesinger, *The Disuniting of America: Reflections on a Multicultural Society* (New York: W. W. Norton & Company, 1992).
[4] Todd Gitlin, *The Twilight of Common dreams: Why America is Wracked by Culture Wars* (New York: Metropolitan Books of Henry Holt and Company, 1995), especially pp. 129-139, and 200-202.
[5] Gitlin, *The Twilight of Common Dreams*, p. 151.
[6] Hollinger, *Postethnic America: Beyond Multiculturalism* (New York: Basic Books, 1995), p. 19.
[7] Frederickson, "America's Diversity in Comparative Perspective," *The Journal of American History* (December 1998), p. 859.
[8] Anthony W. Marx, *Making Race and Nation: A Comparison of South Africa, The*

United States, and Brazil (Cambridge: Cambridge University Press, 1998).

[9] *New York Times*, February 21, 1999.

[10] George Brown Tindall, "Beyond the Mainstream: The Ethnic Southerners," *The Ethnic Southerners* (Baton Rouge: Louisiana State University Press, 1976), pp. 1-21.

[11] See, for instance, Anthony P. Dunbar, *Against The Grain: Southern Radicals and Prophets, 1929-1959* (Charlottesville: University Press of Virginia, 1981), and John Egerton, *Speak Now Against the Day: The Generation Before the Civil Rights Movement in the South* (New York: Knopf, 1994).

[12] Robert Wiebe, *Self-Rule: A Cultural History of American Democracy* (Chicago: The University of Chicago Press, 1995), p. 40.

[13] David Potter, "American Individualism in the Twentieth Century," in Gordon Mills, ed., *Innocence and Power: Individualism in Twentieth Century America* (Austin: University of Texas Press, 1965).

[14] For that argument, see David Leon Chandler, *The Natural Superiority of Southern Politicians: A Revisionist History* (New York: Doubleday and Company, Inc., 1977).

[15] Dan T. Carter, *The Politics of Rage: George Wallace, the Origins of the New Conservatism, and the Transformation of American Politics* (New York: Simon and Schuster, 1995), pp. 466-468.

[16] V. O. Key, Jr., *Southern Politics in State and Nation* (New York: Alfred A. Knopf, 1949). One might also cite C. Vann Woodward's masterful study, *Origins of the New South* (Baton Rouge: Louisiana State University Press, 1951), and more recently John Egerton, *Speak Now Against The Day*.

www.ingramcontent.com/pod-product-compliance
Lightning Source LLC
Chambersburg PA
CBHW050243170426
43202CB00015B/2893